D1116130

TWENTIETH CENTURY
INTERPRETATIONS

MAYNARD MACK, *Series Editor*
Yale University

NOW AVAILABLE
Collections of Critical Essays
ON

THE ADVENTURES OF HUCKLEBERRY FINN

ALL FOR LOVE

THE FROGS

THE GREAT GATSBY

HAMLET

HENRY V

THE ICEMAN COMETH

SAMSON AGONISTES

THE SOUND AND THE FURY

WALDEN

TWENTIETH CENTURY INTERPRETATIONS
OF
TWELFTH NIGHT

TWENTIETH CENTURY INTERPRETATIONS
OF

TWELFTH NIGHT

A Collection of Critical Essays

Edited by
WALTER N. KING

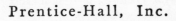Prentice-Hall, Inc. *Englewood Cliffs, N. J.*
A SPECTRUM BOOK

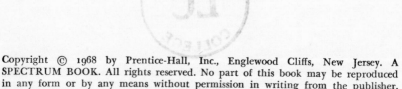

Current printing (last number):
10   9   8   7   6   5   4   3   2   1

Contents

TWENTIETH CENTURY INTERPRETATIONS

OF

TWELFTH NIGHT

Introduction

by Walter N. King

The Shakespeare who composed *Twelfth Night* (1599-1600) was a man a year or two past thirty-five. Behind him stretched a rich and varied decade crammed with personal and professional accomplishment. Actor and shareholder in the Lord Chamberlain's Men, the theatrical company with which he had the luck to become associated in 1594, he was also a poet to be reckoned with and a playwright half of whose achievement in the theater was already completed. By the end of 1594 he had established his reputation as poet with the publication of *Venus and Adonis* (1593) and *The Rape of Lucrece* (1594), and it was already clear that with upwards of ten plays bearing his name (and with Marlowe dead in 1592) he had no serious rivals as a dramatist. Year by year his poetic luster was increasing through manuscript circulation of many of the sonnets, most of which were being written during the 1590's, though this most exciting of all Elizabethan sonnet sequences would not see publication (in a pirated edition) until 1609. Francis Meres was not writing idly, then, when in *Palladis Tamia: Wit's Treasury* (1598) he praised Shakespeare as "mellifluous & hony-tongued" and concluded, somewhat less hyperbolically, "that the Muses would speak with *Shakespeares* fine filed phrases, if they would speak English."

It was Meres, too, who declared that Shakespeare "among the English is the most excellent in both kinds for the stage"—which is to say that by 1598 Shakespeare had, for Meres at least, made himself supreme in both comedy and tragedy. Not uncuriously, of course, considering the average Elizabethan's unwillingness to draw sharp distinctions between genres, among the six tragedies Meres cites (*Richard II, Richard III, Henry IV, King John, Titus Andronicus* and *Romeo and Juliet*—all produced before 1598), four are English history plays, one is vaguely attached to Roman imperial history, while the sixth is set in a more or less contemporary Verona. To this list, after subtracting *Richard III, Henry IV,* and *King John* as scarcely tragic in either vision or tone, we would today add *Julius Caesar* (1599), a genuinely tragic history play unknown to Meres, even though it lacks the abrasive, percussive quality of *Coriolanus* (1607-1609), which as political tragedy it looks forward to. With the advantage of hindsight we can remind ourselves, too, that by 1600 Shakespeare had written nine of the ten English history plays (*Henry VIII* would not appear till 1612-1613) and all nine of the romantic comedies. (I am using the word "romantic" loosely in this introduction.) Hence, we are in no sense surprised that *Hamlet* (1600-1601) followed close upon *Twelfth Night* and may, for all we know, have been under way before *Twelfth Night* was completed and produced. Progression from the one play to the other strikes us as natural and indeed inevitable.

For us *Twelfth Night*'s position as ninth in the series of comedies written during the 1590's, and as the twentieth play in the canon, is more than suggestive. In its underlying melancholy, its nostalgia for something more than mere romantic vision, its search into the nature of human reality (confined in time and space to a planet which the Renaissance intellectual was beginning by 1600 to perceive as only an insignificant part of a universe whose immeasurable vastness was becoming more and more awesome), and yet in its certain faith in human goodness, *Twelfth Night* looks ahead to the great tragedies of the next ten years and to the tragicomic romances with which Shakespeare concluded his career early in the second decade of the seventeenth century. But it is still a funny play. In its gaiety and pace and lyric charm, as well as its satiric exposure of man's folly and pretentiousness, the play is comic through and through and subsumes everything in the comedies that precede it. We can imagine Shakespeare trying one last time to capture, and to articulate perfectly, the mood and tone and content characteristic of the earlier romantic pieces, none of which, not even *As You Like It* (1599-1600), quite catches the essence of Shakespearian romance as it defines itself finally in *Twelfth Night*.

Here again plot is deliberately geared to physical improbability, while thought and sentiment impinge upon, grow out of, comment upon, describe elusively those qualities of human experience we lump together as romantic. Here again occur incidents and plot motifs typical of romance ever since the heyday of the Greek romancers, Heliodorus and Longus. Instance: shipwrecked twins miraculously reunited after an amusing (if threatening) series of mishaps, amusing simply because of Shakespeare's unbounded faith in his audience's "willing suspension of disbelief" when confronted for the umpteenth time with the hackneyed devices of mistaken identity and costume and sex disguise. His was an audience that frankly rejoiced in the nubile young *ingénue,* played by a boy actor, masquerading as a page in the service of a handsome, not-so-intelligent, but eminently lovable leading man whose role requires him to be neither quite in nor out of love—an audience not much different in many respects from the average movie audience whose receptivity to the improbable is one of Hollywood's stablest assets.

In all these plays—leaving aside the Latinate *Comedy of Errors* (1588-1593), Shakespeare's first venture into comedy—love begins at first sight and eventuates in marriage. Everything is, yet is not, erotic. The love theory and conventions of the European Renaissance— Petrarchan, Neoplatonic, Ovidian—are simultaneously spoofed as remote from the amatory realities of the 1590's and clung to as lovely in themselves and therefore not to be cast off lightly simply because experience does not fully square with them. The vagaries of young lovers are everywhere laughed at in the comedies. Their conventionalized phrase-mongering, their erratic sentiments and sentimentalism, their adolescent posturings—all these are made nonsense of by a healthy, always dynamic response to natural impulse which, in their joy and anguish, none of these lovers denies or fails to heed regardless of consequences. Self-fulfillment is their goal, whether they know it or not; love is both end and means, a longed-for tension and a point of rest.

These "harmless follies of the time" Shakespeare submits to the test of a variety of witty value yardsticks, all of them more or less reliable in their opposition to the world of stiffened adult respectabilities and hardening responses to social and religious demands. These latter the lovers resist as if by intuition or at least hold at bay before entering into young adulthood through the broad and beckoning gate of marriage. The tone is always, as C. L. Barber rightly insists, that of holiday balanced perilously against that of workaday[1]—with workaday and holiday gradually coming to terms with each other and with events and people and things, so that a flexible, but insistent compromise brings together youth and age into a graceful sense of community. For love's fulfillment takes place after the play is over. But throughout, the rhythms of human fertility and what it implies for psychic and moral health are being celebrated, whimsy interfused with seriousness, until in the last scenes all comes right, and who cares by what unexpected means?

Our own response is perhaps more inclusive than that of thoughtful Elizabethans. Tuned into time and its passage in ways different from theirs, we sense in Shakespeare's young lovers a perennial resurgence of basic human commitments to emotionality and instinct, each having its own way as always in young people, for whom heart is luckily more important than head. The denouements of the various comedies are simply variations upon each other. They include such episodes as

[1] See *Shakespeare's Festive Comedies* (Princeton, 1959).

wedding playlets, figured dances, masques in honor of Hymen, epitha-
lamia spoken by fairy royalty, and frequently a general departure to
feasting or some other form of hospitable merriment. With Sir James
Frazer behind us we perceive in all these endings clear echoes of
ancient fertility rites long since absorbed into a Christianized civiliza-
tion. And mingled with the joyousness of these occasions we respond as
fully as our ancestors to the profound common sense, the unwailed,
classic knowledge that

> Golden lads and girls all must,
> As chimney-sweepers, come to dust.

These lines, from a much anthologized song in *Cymbeline* (1609-1610),
are a peculiarly suitable epitaph for the comedies of the 1590's—
romantic in tone, realistic in essence.

The fact of mortality is not ignored in *Twelfth Night* ("Come away,
come away, death," Feste sings to Orsino, who is not much pleased
with the song's implied criticism of his own delusive amorousness).
But if death is confined to the background while love spills into every
cranny of the foreground, the reverse is true in *Hamlet* where the
prince grapples with death without remission. Death had already
become existential for Shakespeare; his only son Hamnet had died at
eleven in 1596. With his twin sister Judith, Hamnet had been christened
in the church at Stratford-on-Avon in 1585 when Shakespeare was not
quite twenty-one, and we need to remember that in 1583, when only
nineteen, he had taken his elder daughter Susanna to be christened in
the same church. Shakespeare was a man thrust early into adulthood:
husband at eighteen to a woman apparently eight years older than
he; father of three before he had attained his legal majority; son to
one of Stratford's leading public servants, who appears for reasons of
conscience to have suffered recurrent attacks for recusancy (and been
subjected to heavy fines) from 1577 till well into the 1590's; a supremely
gifted boy for whom perhaps on this account formal university training
was out of the question.

Surely the sadness that surfaces from time to time in *Twelfth Night*
is rooted not only in an ingrained and gradually maturing esthetic
grasp of life, but in experiences tinged early with hardship and
incipient suffering that disclosed how implicated every individual life
is in the realities of pain, mortality, evil. Early on, Shakespeare, ob-
servant and retentive, must have developed his rare capacity for subtle
reflection. He must early have noticed how appearances tend to dis-
tort and deceive and how fools and knaves take advantage of appearances in daily life; how prone to self-delusion, how inclined to
self-destruction, the human psyche is; and how difficult judgment of
any human being becomes as soon as theoretical codes are applied to

individual malefaction. Somewhere within the experiences of adolescence and early manhood, hidden from us owing to almost total lack of intimate biographical documentation (save for the plays and poems which are notoriously difficult to interpret biographically), lie the causes of his habitual double and triple view of situations and especially characters, regarding whom fair and equal judgment is never presented simplified or unshaded. Shakespeare's refusal to be reductive, his most striking trait as a dramatist, must early have become his most striking characteristic as a man.

If in the comedies his outlook upon life is disclosed by means of shifting perspectives, his manipulation of them is not to be taken as mere mannerist habit nor as refusal to judge (a judgment upon Shakespeare common to those who want to judge for him). The endlessly shifting perspectives that substitute for plot in *Twelfth Night*—they might better be called swirling than shifting—are a form of judgment in the making. In the comedies judgment goes on all the time; more often than not it is multiple, not single. It proceeds by means of plot complications, character interaction, twists and turns of theme; by means of symbol and image; by means of witty statement and lyric connotation. This kind of judgment is organic and seems finally to be our own, though in time we begin to sense that we ourselves have been caught up in the rearranging perspectives as thoroughly as the characters. By the conclusion of *Twelfth Night* we feel certain what our judgment of the play is, only to discover during our next experience with it that our former judgment has veered away from what it used to be. Yet repeated experiences with this, or with any of the major comedies, confirm what we are sure we have known all the time: what it is that Shakespeare fundamentally believes, what he can do without, what he would improve upon if he could, what he holds fast to regardless of price.

It is Shakespeare's judgment in the making that gives to the literature upon *Twelfth Night* the quality pervasive to the play: elusiveness. Those who write critically upon it agree in the main with those who have already had their say or will have it tomorrow. Yet at some critical point, as the essays in this volume demonstrate, each critic assumes a stance fully his own. Criticism of *Twelfth Night,* being a criticism of changing perspectives and reaction to the change, is finally perspectivist. How could it be otherwise when without rancor critics disagree about which of the so-called plots is primary, about which of the leading characters is central, about which of the themes is the nucleus around which the others cohere? Toward which character is our empathy most intensely directed? To Olivia or to Viola? To Malvolio? Or to Feste? Is the play just an amorous romp that eventually leads to the pairing off of Jack with Jill, of Joan with John? Or is it a serious,

though laughter-filled, representation of issues relevant not only to the
early seventeenth century, when so many serious issues were aborning,
but also the twentieth? For instance, the problem of identity, about
which I will have more to say further on.

Not that criticism of *Twelfth Night* is individualistic or cantankerous
or vaguely cognitive; it is in the best sense noncontroversial. Opinions
on minor issues differ, but everyone knows what the play is "about";
indeed, criticism of it exemplifies almost categorically Eliot's remark
in "The Function of Criticism" that the critic's business is "the elucida-
tion of works of art and the correction of taste." Naturally enough, the
changing perspectives within the play appear different to different
critics, whose own perspectives vary according to subjective bias, to
"what you will." But they do not vary enough to prompt debate, nig-
gling or otherwise, about cruces of one sort or another, as has happened, for instance, in the criticism of *Hamlet* and in plays like *Troilus
and Cressida* and *Measure for Measure*—all of them products of the
early 1600's. It is perspectivist criticism almost entirely and as such is
securely anchored in a metaphor of perspectives stated openly by Orsino early in Act V.

II

Let me begin exploration of this metaphor by quoting Feste's rather
acid comment in Act V to Malvolio, for whom the prospect of changed
perspectives has led to folly heaped on folly: "And thus the whirligig
of time brings in its revenges." Implicit here is the metaphor of perspectives which earlier in the act, after the revelation that Viola and
Sebastian are identical twins, had been voiced openly in Orsino's
wondering exclamation:

> One face, one voice, one habit, and two persons!
> A natural perspective, that is and is not!

Momentarily perspectives congeal and percipient spectators become
aware that Shakespeare's apparent trifling with optical illusion has
all along been something more than self-indulgence. With the discovery that Cesario is both Viola *and* Sebastian, not just a disguise or an
identity mistaken, characters guilty of deceiving others or themselves
or both can now perhaps enjoy a fundamental change of perspective.
For Olivia and Orsino, Viola and Sebastian (the only major character
undisguised throughout), change of perspective is educative in a per-
manent sense. Experiential and therefore natural, changing perspectives have produced the disclosure that paradoxically two can be one,
and yet remain two; that a thing can be, yet not-be simultaneously;

and that permeating the disorder and confusion typical of experience is an order that reveals itself only because perspectives do change. So much for characters who have eyes that see. For characters whose eyes remain closed, or half shut (like Sir Toby, Sir Andrew, and Malvolio) changing perspectives fail to enlighten. Instead they obfuscate and lead with the force of predestination to the revenges administered by time. For Malvolio, a determined withdrawal into the self he has loved too much; for Sir Toby, a broken head and marriage to a woman capable of confining him "within the modest limits of order"; for Sir Andrew, a continuation of the gentlemanly asininity he was born into.

How seriously we take Shakespeare's metaphor of perspectives depends upon our familiarity with seventeenth century meanings of "perspective." Abstractly, the term implied then, as it does now, "a mental view, outlook, or prospect," or "the action of looking into something, close inspection, insight or penetrativeness" (see the *OED*). Concretely, the term had precise technical meanings as used in the developing science of optics and in Renaissance painting, in which the art of perspective, especially linear perspective, had reached its culmination long since. Specifically, a "perspective" was "a picture or figure constructed so as to produce some fantastic effect; e.g., appearing distorted or confused except from one particular point of view, or presenting totally different aspects from different points" (again, see the *OED*). Orsino uses the word in this technical sense when he describes Viola and Sebastian as "a natural perspective"—that is, a perspective created by nature as technician, not by man.

Shakespeare's use of the term in this sense is consistent with his practice elsewhere. In *Richard II* (1595) Bushy remarks to Richard's foreboding queen:

> For sorrow's eyes, glazed with blinding tears,
> Divide one thing entire to many objects,
> Like perspectives, which rightly [i.e., frontally] gaz'd upon,
> Show nothing but confusion—ey'd awry,
> Distinguish form.   (II.ii.16-20)

And in *All's Well* (1602-1604) Bertram, extenuating his caddish behavior toward Helena, leans on the same image, though in addition to emphasis upon distortions deliberately contrived for a painting, he relies on normal contemporary usage of "perspective" to mean an optical glass capable of producing a distorted image (again, see the *OED*):

> At first
> I struck my choice upon her, ere my heart
> Durst make too bold a herald of my tongue:
> Where the impression of mine eye infixing,

> Contempt his scornful perspective did lend me,
> Which warped the line of every other favor,
> Scorned a fair color or expressed it stol'n,
> Extended or contracted all proportions
> To a most hideous object.   (V.iii.44-52)

Here the term, developed in a semimetaphysical way, focuses squarely upon the comic issue of failure to maintain proportion, something Orsino, with the whole of the play's action behind him, scarcely needs to imply. After all, as a play in which perspectives are of all sorts, *Twelfth Night* can be likened in the way its "meanings" ramify outward in unexpected and provocative directions to an elaborately developed metaphysical conceit.

The play begins with everything out of proportion (the play's term for it is "excess"). The Twelfth Night atmosphere of the Lord of Misrule, about which everyone comments, is of course the atmosphere of excess, but it is holiday excess, which from one perspective is its own justification. Yet even holiday excess, imaged in the nightly revels of Sir Toby and his cronies, becomes a kind of defect when it encroaches upon everyday and workaday, so that in Malvolio is imaged a counter excess which also breeds its own defect: the human need for orderliness, which Sir Toby scorns and which Malvolio carries too far. Orderliness is an everyday virtue, to be sure, but it is seldom admired by the generously permissive, whether in 1600 or today. Nevertheless it is admired by Olivia, who rebukes Malvolio for self-love, but depends upon him as steward of her household for a regulated domestic economy. The trouble is that Malvolio's virtue is not just excessive; it is a psychological disguise that ineffectually conceals the pernicious disorder of social climbing. For this reason the case for order appears weaker than the case for revelry, whose strength is epitomized once and for all in Sir Toby's epigrammatic retort to Malvolio: "Dost thou think, because thou art virtuous, there shall be no more cakes and ale?" No doubt, Sir Toby's credo, expressed early in the play, ". . . care's an enemy to life," deserves more than a once-a-week sermon. But no case in *Twelfth Night* is ever fully closed. Perspectives alter. With Sir Toby's first belch, revelry as a way of life seems somehow less appealing. Cakes and ale need not be done without, nor will they ever be, but too many of them? Sir Toby will not stay for an answer.

Somewhere, then, between these two forms of excess and defect exists a proper standard for tolerable human conduct. Feste presumably knows what it is, but admonition in him is always oblique or quibbling, as if wisdom can be learned only from experience. And experience alone is decisive for those suffering from the distempers attendant upon love. Malvolio's self-love amounts to outrageous excess synonymous with outrageous defect. Presumably Olivia's and Orsino's sentimental responses to affection should also be so judged. That they are not—that in each, excess does not become defect—is a sure gauge of Shakespeare's grasp of the dynamic of perspectivism. It is noticeable that neither character can be reduced to a single quality definable by an appropriate name. Available to each are perspectives broader than those available to Malvolio or Sir Toby, and so in spite of excessive divagation in their reaction to love's natural promptings, each is self-educable through changes of perspective—which is what experience amounts to for both. Given sufficient shift in psychological pressures—and this is Viola's role vis-à-vis each—each of them begins naturally to reach outward from self (in both a synonym for excess) to the qualities each seeks in the person known to both as Cesario. In Olivia this process is self-conscious and deliberate from the start. In Orsino it remains largely unconscious till the end, but is nonetheless total. Natural perspectives propel each in the direction he wishes to go, and if each reaches outward from self toward union with Cesario, each is concurrently discovering what love is and is not, and each is discovering who he is and what he wants.

"What are you? What would you?" Olivia asks Viola-Cesario during their first encounter and thereby initiates a pattern of questioning that extends into Act V. These two questions, or variations of them, are in fact the radical questions of the play. Implied answers to them depend upon the perspective of the moment and range from the obvious to the riddling (see especially Viola's various comments to Olivia about her own and Olivia's identity) to the philosophically subtle (see Feste's not-so-nonsensical comments upon his own identity in the Sir Topas scene). Who one is seems to vary as perspectives vary. Yet Olivia is always Olivia, Viola is always Viola, Sebastian and Orsino are always themselves in ways that illustrate the psychology and metaphysic implicit in Orsino's puzzled "a natural perspective, that is and is not." [2]

Who you are depends rather substantially upon "what you will" (that is, upon "what would you?"). Shakespeare's subtitle—the only one in the canon—turns out to be unexpectedly meaningful. On a superficial view it means no more than "whatever you please." But "will" in Shakespeare's English could be punned upon in multiple ways. "Will" could mean simple volition or intention, moral choice, sheer willfulness, carnal desire, even the genitals—male or female. And "will" was commonly thought of in antithesis to "wit" (i.e., reason employed with integrity). Only by implication is this antithesis verbally

alive in *Twelfth Night,* but Feste's witty exposure of Olivia's and Orsino's folly belongs to the tradition. It is, of course, fully dramatized
in Malvolio's reflexive monologue upon the forged letter he assumes
Olivia has dropped in his way:

> M,O,A,I. This simulation [disguised meaning] is not as the former. And
> yet, to crush [force] this a little, it would bow to me, for every one of
> these letters are in my name.

Here "wit" is coolly defeated by "will," and in the process Malvolio is
exposed as the self-interested moral fraud Maria has already stated he
is.

In this scene perspectives shift in bewildering swirls that suggest
how intimately the human will is associated with changing perspectives
and how rapidly signal changes in perspective set new perspectives in
motion. "What you will," it becomes evident, depends to a large degree upon who you are, and "what you will" prompts willful choices
in other people. These in turn prompt additional perspectives. By the
end of Act III volitions, choices, desires begin to engulf each other until character after character feels awash in what Olivia calls "midsummer madness." Characters engaged in deception or self-deception begin
to lose their ability to cope, while characters like Antonio and the Sea
Captain, in whom simple integrity is the major trait, find it tempora-
rily a liability. Only Sebastian, undisguised and analytical even in the
midst of the comic vortex, is able to keep afloat and wait without anxiety for enlightenment.

It comes ironically with the disclosure that as one entity in a "natural perspective," he and Viola are *both* Cesario, though both possess
independent identities. On the other hand, whatever Cesario is beyond
his confusing doubleness, "he" has identity enough to attract not only
Olivia, but Orsino and rouse the best qualities in both. Twentieth
century audiences boggle at the paradoxes implied in this equation—
in particular the implication that unity and duality may not be dis-
tinct concepts, as we like to think, and may in fact be different aspects
of the same thing. But this metaphysical possibility is surely no harder
to understand than Donne's paradox in "A Valediction: Forbidding
Mourning":

> Our two souls therefore, which are one,
>   Though I must goe, endure not yet
> A breach, but an expansion,
>   Like gold to ayery thinnesse beate.

Implicit also in the "natural perspective" of identical twins, one male,
one female, is an attitude toward sexual differentiation (I shall be
more explicit about it in a moment) that should trouble no thoughtful

spectator in the twentieth century. Here let me state only that it is not a matter of latent homosexuality in Orsino or Olivia that attracts both to Cesario, nor of hermaphroditic tendencies in either or in Viola, as one recent avant-garde production of the play insisted upon.

Sebastian offers the beginning of an explanation when he remarks wittily to Olivia in Act V:

> So comes it, lady, you have been mistook.
> But nature to her bias drew in that.

Nature, the very ordering principle in the universe, says Sebastian, is responsible for Orsino's and Olivia's mistake-that-is-not-a-mistake, and nature he images as an outdoor bowler casting his bowling ball obliquely down the green according to the bias, or curve, built into the ball itself. Nature, in other words, has presented Orsino and Olivia with a perspective, an opportunity for choice, that shakes the two of them out of the sentimentalism that was, in effect, a denial of life and shoves them into head-on confrontation with it.

In his need for love Orsino has been reaching outward, naturally but obliquely, for the sense of purpose that only love can bring to his kind of man. Purpose he associates vaguely with femininity (see his confidential man-to-man talks with Cesario on man and woman in love), a trait common to both Olivia and Viola. The latter's feminine appeal is enhanced, not hidden, by costume and sex disguise and is indeed one of the psychological realities typical of adolescence, regardless of sex. Orsino's apparently sudden acceptance of Viola as beloved and wife-to-be is simply emblematic of what today we call the shock of recognition, the moment of truth.

Similarly, in her need for love Olivia has been reaching outward for new perspectives. She finds them in the forthright, confident masculinity Viola imitates in her masquerade as Cesario, a masculinity modeled upon qualities prominent in Sebastian from the moment he enters the action and latent in Viola as identical twin to Sebastian. The superficial improbability that upsets modern audiences in Olivia's transfer of affection from Viola to Sebastian is actually a red herring situation. Depth psychology tells us that differentiation between masculinity and femininity in adolescence is seldom absolute and that basic sexual characteristics are capable of considerable overlap, not only in adolescence but throughout life. (We should bear in mind that Viola and Sebastian, Olivia and Orsino are all young people enjoying late adolescence or very early adulthood.)

Shakespeare seems to have anticipated some such theoretical conclusion. But with the device of identical twins, which he inherited from Plautine comedy and had ten years earlier given a preliminary workout in *The Comedy of Errors,* he was working emblematically.

Cesario is an amalgam of the most attractive traits of both Viola and Sebastian. Genuine love, instinctive but not necessarily directionless, comes about in Olivia and Orsino precisely because of those traits in Cesario most appealing to each, but they are traits shared by Viola and Sebastian as identical twins. In short, the metaphor "a natural perspective, that is and is not" is really a kind of metaphysical conceit which the entire play has been dramatizing. Viola and Sebastian, both of whom are Cesario, are emblems of a metaphysical possibility—that oneness cannot be so easily distinguished from twoness as human beings like to think; and of a psychological reality—that Olivia and Orsino fell in love with given human personalities far more than with given human bodies. To an age like the Renaissance, firm in its conviction that love cannot be reduced to a simplified vision of sex, but willing to give sex its due, Shakespeare's conceit would not have seemed extravagant. Nor would it have been literalized into an unacceptable improbability as modern audiences tend to do.

III

I have brought to *Twelfth Night* this perspectivist point of view to suggest a conclusion appropriate to all the critical interpretations printed in this volume: that the play opens outward to a variety of interpretations, no one of which outlaws any other, and all of which complement one another. Critics take more or less for granted the proposition that Shakespeare's major concern is with humanity's controlling needs for holiday, for a regularized existence that includes workaday, and for the joys and pains of love—all of which require healthy outlets lest they find outlets injurious to self and to one's fellows. All this may seem overly solemn for a play brimming with high spirits, especially a play called *Twelfth Night*. True enough, the Twelve Days of Christmas were traditionally spent in revelry, much of it boisterous, but Twelfth Night, when the pleasures of misrule culminated, was also conceived of as prologue to Epiphany, a festival day consecrated to Christ as symbol and essence of all ordering principles. Hence, man's controlling needs are peculiarly available to Twelfth Night treatment and judgment, to an alternation from gaiety to sobriety. Yet it is significant that never in *Twelfth Night* does Shakespeare provide a recipe giving specific instruction how holiday, ordered principles, and fulfillment of self through love should combine proportionately in the shaping of any individual life. His refusal to be didactic in any schoolmasterly fashion is a tribute to his rare common sense, to his faith in "what you will." The comedies of the nineties are, of course, indirectly didactic (what art worth troubling about is not?), but as works of art they inform us *directly* more about how Shakespeare developed a comic vision responsive to human needs and aspirations, and gradually worked out a form suitable to its ambivalent expression, than about what that vision is. It was a process that included mastering conventional types of comedy already on the boards at the beginning of his career, exploiting their possibilities to the limit of his own imaginative powers and eventually creating a form of comedy characteristically his own which attained perfection in *Twelfth Night*.

That the play was popular in its own time we need not doubt. So far as we know, it was never published in quarto form, good presumptive evidence that for Shakespeare's company it remained marketable in the theater for a long time. It was revived early in the Restoration. Pepys viewed it three times between 1660 and 1668, "though it be but a silly play, and not related at all to the name or day" (see the diary entry for 6 January, 1662/3). There is no need, of course, to bow before the middlebrow judgment of Pepys. We would do better to assume that Shakespeare's critical concern with the relationship of appearance to reality, which ramifies further in *Twelfth Night* than many Shakespearians of today care to believe, placed it for astute seventeenth century spectators within the boundaries of mannerist relevance—along with *Hamlet*. Certainly the ambivalent handling of the love theme sets the play well within the Renaissance dialogue about love's nature, both its perverse and natural expressions, which continued far into the seventeenth century, while Shakespeare's preoccupation with conduct links it with the on-going ethical concerns of humanism.

Whether the play is relevant for those of us living in the midtwentieth century is less easy to decide. As a document for cultural historians and historians of ideas, *Twelfth Night* has its uses. But leaving aside its cultural value and ignoring the remnants of bardolatry which still persist in people for whom anything by Shakespeare is *ipso facto* worth gold mines, it might plausibly be argued that aside from its fun and the lightheartedness with which it can be played by vintage actors, the play has little to offer an age alleged to be locked in a death struggle with metaphysical *angst*, yet naïve enough to assume that the camera antics of *Blow-Up* are a profound commentary upon man's plight. Neither has *Twelfth Night* much to offer those for whom love as a literary theme must be knotted in repression and cast in Oedipal tonalities. But dismissal of the play on these counts is surely premature. Relevant or not to "the age of anxiety," *Twelfth Night* is still frequently revived in England and America, both in academic localities and in the professional theaters, where it is given a wide swathe of interpretations usually provocative and often provoking.

The play has, in fact, its own kind of relevance to dominant attitudes of our time. Feste's wry comments on his world—its stupidity, folly, disvalue—suggest a willingness to opt out, and his final no-nonsense song insists upon what happens to those who opt out in the wrong way. This is not to say that Shakespeare is anticipating Kierkegaard or Nietzsche or Heidegger. For Shakespeare existence does not precede essence, nor does value depend upon contemporaneity. But in his treatment of the problem of identity, overtly in *The Comedy of Errors* and *Twelfth Night,* undercover in other comedies (see Antonio's opening lines in *The Merchant of Venice*: "In sooth I know not why I am so sad./It wearies me, you say it wearies you. . . ."), Shakespeare is moving with the main stream of his own age and casting light upon ours. Significantly, Shakespeare can make incisive comment upon identity within a frame of reference still orthodox; many in our age who comment upon this issue assume blandly that to do so with any cogency demands a total break with orthodoxy. Nevertheless, when we compare Shakespeare's way with those common to us, it is chastening to realize that, like him, we are still asking Olivia's questions to Viola: "Who are you? What would you?", and we are still coping with natural perspectives that are and are not. Our coping tools, we like to think, are more numerous and more finely honed than Shakespeare's. Perhaps they are, but we need to ask from time to time whether the use we put them to provides answers to Olivia's questions more finely honed than those implied in Shakespeare's play.

In *Twelfth Night* the complexity of man's response to his world is in the foreground throughout and is judged in relation to man's possibilities for good. This we would expect in any significant older comedy. In *Hamlet* and the succeeding tragedies, man's complexity of response is multiplied in breadth and depth, but it is still conceived and judged, in spite of Shakespeare's confrontation with evil and despair, in terms of man's possibilities for good. This we might not expect. But it is typical of the Judaeo-Christian ethic, in relation to which all of Shakespeare's comedies and tragedies were written, once it had been transformed by the humanistic speculations of men like Montaigne and, let us admit it, by Shakespeare himself. The very questions Olivia asks are tersely descriptive, in terms of intellectual history, of man's descent into himself, there to study his own ambiguous nature. Indeed, when Viola replies to Olivia, "I am not what I am," her riddling comment heralds the beginning of an introspective movement whose culmination in Freud and Jung and their disciples in our century none of us can ignore. A world in which, to make any sense, man must view himself as part of a "natural perspective"—and this is Shakespeare's mental world by 1600—is no longer the reductive world of Shakespeare's youth and young manhood. It is a world already facing toward whatever it is we mean when we use the term "modern."

The Masks of *Twelfth Night*

by Joseph H. Summers

Love and its fulfillment are primary in Shakespeare's comedies. Its conflicts are often presented in terms of the battle of the generations. At the beginning of the plays the bliss of the young lovers is usually barred by an older generation of parents and rulers, a group which has supposedly experienced its own fulfillment in the past and which is now concerned with preserving old forms or fulfilling new ambitions. The comedies usually end with the triumph in which the lovers make peace with their elders and themselves assume adulthood and often power. The revolutionary force of love becomes an added element of vitality in a reestablished society.

Twelfth Night does not follow the customary pattern. In this play the responsible older generation has been abolished, and there are no parents at all. In the first act we are rapidly introduced into a world in which the ruler is a love-sick Duke—in which young ladies, fatherless and motherless, embark on disguised actions, or rule, after a fashion, their own households, and in which the only individuals possibly over thirty are drunkards, jokesters, and gulls, totally without authority. All the external barriers to fulfillment have been eliminated in what becomes almost a parody of the state desired by the ordinary young lovers, the Hermias and Lysanders—or even the Rosalinds and Orlandos. According to the strictly romantic formula, the happy ending should be already achieved at the beginning of the play: we should abandon the theater for the rites of love. But the slightly stunned inhabitants of Illyria discover that they are anything but free. Their own actions provide the barriers, for most of them know neither themselves, nor others, nor their social worlds.

For his festival entertainment, Shakespeare freshly organized all the usual material of the romances—the twins, the exile, the impersona-

"*The Masks of* Twelfth Night" *by Joseph H. Summers. From* The University Review, XXII (*1955*), 25-32. Copyright © *1955 by the University of Missouri at Kansas City. Reprinted by permission of* The University Review.

tions—to provide significant movement for a dance of maskers. Every character has his mask, for the assumption of the play is that no one is without a mask in the seriocomic business of the pursuit of happiness. The character without disguises who is not ridiculous is outside the realm of comedy. Within comedy, the character who thinks it is possible to live without assuming a mask is merely too naïve to recognize the mask he has already assumed. He is the chief object of laughter. As a general rule, we laugh with the characters who know the role they are playing and we laugh at those who do not; we can crudely divide the cast of *Twelfth Night* into those two categories.

But matters are more complicated than this, and roles have a way of shifting. All the butts except perhaps Sir Andrew Aguecheek have moments in which they appear as fools. In our proper confusion, we must remember the alternative title of the play, "What You Will." It may indicate that everyone is free to invent his own title for the proceedings. It also tells the author's intention to fulfill our desires: we wish to share in the triumphs of love and we wish to laugh; we wish our fools occasionally to be wise, and we are insistent that our wisest dramatic figures experience our common fallibility. Most significantly, the title may hint that what "we" collectively "will" creates all the comic masks—that society determines the forms of comedy more directly than it determines those of any other literary genre.

At the opening of the play Orsino and Olivia accept the aristocratic (and literary) ideas of the romantic lover and the grief-stricken lady as realities rather than as ideas. They are comic characters exactly because of that confusion. Orsino glories in the proper moodiness and fickleness of the literary lover; only our own romanticism can blind us to the absurdities in his opening speech. Orsino first wishes the music to continue so that the appetite of love may "surfeit"; immediately, however, he demands that the musicians stop the music they are playing to repeat an isolated phrase—an awkward procedure and a comic bit of stage business which is rarely utilized in productions. Four lines later the music must stop entirely because the repeated "strain" no longer *is* sweet, and the appetite is truly about to "surfeit." He then exclaims that the spirit of love is so "quick and fresh" that like the sea (hardly a model of freshness)

> naught enters there,
> Of what validity and pitch soe'er,
> But falls into abatement and low price,
> Even in a minute!

Orsino is a victim of a type of madness to which the most admirable characters are sometimes subject. Its usual causes are boredom, lack of physical love, and excessive imagination, and the victim is unaware that he is in love with love rather than with a person.

In the same scene, before we ever see the lady, Olivia's state is as nicely defined. Valentine, Orsino's messenger, has acquired something of his master's extraordinary language, and his report on his love mission manages both to please the Duke and to convey his own incredulity at the excess of Olivia's vow for her brother. In his speech the fresh and the salt are again confused. It is impossible to keep fresh something so ephemeral as grief; Olivia can make it last and "season" it, however, by the process of pickling—the natural effect of "eye-of-fending brine." Orsino feels unbounded admiration for the depth of soul indicated by Olivia's vow and at the same time he assumes that the vow can easily be broken by a lover. He departs for "sweet *beds* of flow'rs" which are somehow to provide a *canopy* for "love-thoughts."

Both Orsino and Olivia have adopted currently fashionable literary postures; yet neither of them is a fool. We are glad to be reassured by the Captain that Orsino is "A noble duke, in nature as in name," and that his present infatuation is only a month old. Sir Toby's later remark "What a plague means my niece, to take the death of her brother thus?" indicates that Olivia too had seemed an unlikely candidate for affectation. She is also an unconvincing practitioner. Although at our first glimpse of her she is properly the grief-stricken lady ("Take the fool away"), her propriety collapses under Feste's famous catechism. We discover that Olivia is already bored and that she really desires to love. Outraged nature has its full and comic revenge when Olivia falls passionately in love with a male exterior and acts with an aggressiveness which makes Orsino seem almost feminine. Still properly an actor in comedy, Olivia quickly changes from the character who has confused herself with a socially attractive mask to one which society has imposed on another.

Viola's situation allows time for neither love- nor grief-in-idleness. A virgin, shipwrecked in a strange land, possessing only wit and intelligence and the Captain's friendship, she must act immediately if she is to preserve herself. She, like Olivia, has "lost" a brother, but the luxury of conventional mourning is quickly exchanged for a *willed* hope that, as she was saved, "so perchance may he be." With Viola's wish for time to know what her "estate is," before she is "delivered to the world," we are reminded that society often requires a mask, neither for the relief of boredom nor the enjoyment of acting, but merely for self-preservation. While Antonio, "friend to Sebastian," almost loses his life because of his failure to assume a disguise, Viola suffers from no failure of discretion or imagination. She must assume a disguise as a boy and she must have help in preparing it.

Although she knows the ways of the world, Viola takes the necessary chance and wills to trust the Captain:

> There is a fair behavior in thee, Captain.
> And though that Nature with a beauteous wall
> Doth oft close in pollution, yet of thee
> I will believe thou hast a mind that suits
> With this thy fair and outward character.

We have in this second scene not only the beginning of one strand of the complicated intrigue, but also the creation of the one character active in the intrigue who provides a measure for the comic excesses of all the others. (Feste's role as observer is analogous to Viola's role as "actor.") Although Viola chooses to impersonate Cesario from necessity, she later plays her part with undisguised enjoyment. She misses none of the opportunities for parody, for confession, and for *double entendre* which the mask affords, and she never forgets or lets us forget the biological distance between Viola and Cesario. Except in the fencing match with Sir Andrew Aguecheek, she anticipates and directs our perception of the ludicrous in her own role as well as in the roles of Orsino and Olivia.

Sebastian is the reality of which Cesario is the artful imitation. Viola's twin assumes no disguises; Viola and the inhabitants of Illyria have assumed it for him. He is, to the eye, identical with Viola, and his early scenes with Antonio serve to remind us firmly of his existence as well as to introduce an initial exhilarating confusion at the entrance of either of the twins. When he truly enters the action of the play in Act IV he is certainly the object of our laughter, not because he has confused himself with an ideal or improper mask, but because he so righteously and ineffectually insists on his own identity in the face of unanimous public opposition. Out attitude quickly changes, however, to a mixture of amused patronization and identification: we do, after all, *know* so much more than does Sebastian; yet, within the context of the play, we can hardly keep from identifying with the gentleman who, practically if not idealistically, decides not to reject the reality of a passionate Olivia just because he has never seen her before:

> Or I am mad, or else this is a dream.
> Let fancy still my sense in Lethe steep.
> If it be thus to dream, still let me sleep!

The other characters in the play do not truly belong to an aristocracy of taste and leisure. For some of them, that is the chief problem. Malvolio and Sir Andrew Aguecheek are ruled by their mistaken notions of the proper role of an upper-class gentleman, and they fail to perceive the comic gaps between themselves and their ideal roles,

and between those ideals and the social reality. Sick with self-love as
he is, Malvolio is also sick with his desire to rise in society: "an affectioned ass, that cons state without book and utters it by great swaths:
the best persuaded of himself, so crammed, as he thinks, with ex-
cellencies, that it is his grounds of faith that all that look on him love
him." Although he knows it without, he has learned his "state" by
book—but such a pupil inevitably distorts the text. He dreams of rul-
ing a thrifty and solemn household while he plays with "some rich
jewel," a dream characteristically attractive to the *arriviste* and
absolutely impossible to the *arrivé*. We, like Maria, "can hardly forbear hurling things at him." His is as absurd as the reverse image
which possesses Sir Andrew, a carpet-knight rightly described by Sir
Toby as "an ass-head and a coxcomb and a knave, a thin-faced knave,
a gull!" In the gallery of false images Sir Andrew's roaring boy hangs
opposite Malvolio's burgher. Although in a low moment Sir Andrew
may think that he has "no more wit than a Christian or an ordinary
man has," he never has such grave self-doubt for long. Like a true gull,
he tries to assume the particular role which, of all others, he is most
poorly equipped to play: drinker, fighter, wencher.

Sir Andrew, however, would hardly exist without Sir Toby Belch:
the gull must have his guller. Sir Toby may fulfill Sir Andrew's idea
of what a gentleman should be, but Sir Toby himself has no such odd
idea of gentility. (Sir Andrew may be "a dear manikin to you, Sir
Toby," but Sir Toby has a superlatively good reason for allowing him
to be: "I have been dear to him, lad, some two thousand strong, or so.")
Even at his most drunken, we are delightfully unsure whether we laugh
at or with Sir Toby, whether he is or is not fully conscious of the effects
as well as the causes of his "mistakes," his verbal confusions, and even
his belches. Like another drunken knight, and like Viola, Toby possesses a range of dramatic talents and he enjoys using them. He is equally
effective as the fearless man of action, as the practitioner of noble
"gentleness' with the "mad" Malvolio, and as the experienced alcoholic
guide to Sir Andrew. His joy is in the jest as well as in the bottle, and
he can bring himself to abandon the latter long enough to marry
Maria simply in admiration for her ability as an intriguer. But like
other knowing players, Sir Toby is vulnerable to deception. He is
object rather than master of our laughter from the time when he
mistakes Sebastian for Cesario and attempts to assert his masculine
ability as a swordsman.

In the business of masking, Feste is the one professional among a
crowd of amateurs; he does it for a living. He never makes the amateur's
mistake of confusing his personality with his mask—he wears not
motley in his brain. Viola recognizes his wisdom and some kinship in
the fact that each "must observe their mood on whom he jests." But

though Feste may have deliberately chosen his role, society determines its conditions. Now that he is growing old, the conditions become difficult: "Go to, you're a dry fool, I'll no more of you. Besides, you grow dishonest." While all the other characters are concerned with gaining something they do not have, Feste's struggle is to retain his mask and to make it again ingratiating. He is able to penetrate all the masks of the others, and he succeeds in retaining his own.

However fanciful its dreams of desire, the play moves within a context of an almost real world, from one disguise and half-understood intrigue to another, until all its elements are whirled into a complexly related and moving figure. With the constant contrasts and parallels and reversals in character, situation, and intrigue we find ourselves at last, along with Malvolio and Olivia and Viola and the rest, in a state of real delirium. Until the concluding scene, however, we can largely agree with Sebastian: if we dream, we do not wish to wake; if this is madness, it is still comic madness, and we do not envy the sane. The attempts at false and inflexible authority are being defeated, the pretentious are being deflated, and the very sentimentality of the likeable sentimentalists has led them close to biological reality. We are particularly delighted with Viola. Young, intelligent, zestful, she is a realist. She cuts through the subterfuges and disguises of the others with absolute clarity, and she provides us with a center for the movement, a standard or normality which is never dull. In her rejection of the artificial myths of love, moreover, Viola never becomes the advocate of a far more terrifying myth, the myth of absolute rationality. In a completely rational world, Shakespeare never tires of pointing out, what we know as love could not exist. We have never desired such a world.

From the time of her first aside to the audience after she has seen Orsino ("Yet a barful strife!/Whoe'er I woo, myself would be his wife"), Viola directly admits her irrational love. She differs, then, from Orsino and Olivia not in any invulnerability to blindness and passion, but in the clarity and simplicity with which she recognizes and accepts her state. Reason is not abandoned: she rationally admits her irrationality and her inability to cope with the situation:

> O Time, thou must untangle this, not I!
> It is too hard a knot for me to untie!

Viola needs a miracle. Although she may imagine herself as "Patience on a monument, smiling at grief," she remains as close as possible to her loved one and waits for the miracle to happen. Since we have seen Sebastian, we know that the miracle will occur; yet through our identification with Viola we come to know the comic burden, the masker's increasing weariness of the mask which implies that love is still pursued rather than possessed.

The burden becomes comically unbearable only in the final scene, when it is cast off. Here Shakespeare underscores all those possibilities of violence and death which are usually submerged in comedy. Antonio is arrested and in danger of his life. Orsino, finally recognizing the hopelessness of his suit to Olivia, shows the vicious side of sentimentality. After considering the possibility of killing Olivia "like to the Egyptian thief," he determines to do violence to "Cesario:"

> Come, boy, with me. My thoughts are
> ripe in michief.
> I'll sacrifice the lamb that I do love,
> To spite a raven's heart within a dove.

Olivia is hysterical at what seems to be the baseness of Cesario. Sir Toby has a broken pate to show for his one major failure to penetrate a mask. The dance must stop. The miracle must occur.

The entrance of Sebastian is "what we will." It is the most dramatic moment of the play. The confrontation of Sebastian and Cesario-Viola, those identical images, concludes the formal plot and provides the means for the discarding of all the lovers' masks. The moment must be savored and fully realized. As Viola and Sebastian chant their traditional formulas of proof, both the audience and the other characters on the stage undistractedly view the physical image of the duality which has made the confusion and the play. The masks and the play are to be abandoned for a vision of delight beyond delight, in which lovers have neither to wear nor to penetrate disguises since they are at last invulnerable to error and laughter.

Yet the play does not resolve into a magic blessing of the world's fertility as does *A Midsummer Night's Dream.* We have been promised a happy ending, and we receive it. We are grateful that the proper Jacks and Jills have found each other, but the miracle is a limited miracle, available only to the young and the lucky. Not every Jack has his Jill even in Illyria, and after the general unmasking, those without love may seem even lonelier. Malvolio, of course, is justly punished. He has earned his mad scene, and with the aid of Feste he has made it comic. As a result of his humiliation he has also earned some sort of redress. Yet he is ridiculous in his arrogance to the end, and his threatened revenge, now that he is powerless to effect it, sustains the comedy and the characterization and prevents the obtrusion of destructive pathos.

It is Feste rather than Malvolio who finally reminds us of the limitations and the costs of the romantic vision of happiness with which we have been seduced. However burdensome, masking is his career, and romantic love provides no end for it. Alone on the stage at the end of the play, he sings a song of unfulfilled love which shows the other side of the coin. For Feste, as for his audience, the mask can never be finally discarded: the rain it raineth every day. His song has those overtones, I believe, but they are only overtones. The music, here and elsewhere in the play, provides an element in which oppositions may be resolved. And the song itself, like the movement which must accompany it, is crude and witty as well as graceful and nostalgic. However far it may have missed the conventionally happy ending, Feste's saga of misfortunes in love is comic, even from his own point of view. The exaggeration so often operative in the refrains of Elizabethan lyrics emphasizes that the watery as well as the sunny vision can become funny: it doesn't rain every day by a long shot.

The song, which begins as the wittiest observer's comment on the denouement of the play, ends as a dissolution of the dramatic fiction:

> A great while ago the world begun,
>   With hey, ho, the wind and the rain,
> But that's all one, our play is done,
>   And we'll strive to please you every day.

The audience has been a participant in the festivity. As the fictional lovers have unmasked to reveal or realize their "true" identities, it is only proper that the clown, the only character who might move freely in the environs of Bankside, as well as in the realm of Illyria, should unmask the whole proceeding for the imitation of a desired world which it has been. The audience must be returned from "What You Will" to its own less patterned world where the sea rarely disgorges siblings given up for lost, where mistaken marriages rarely turn out well, where Violas rarely catch Dukes, and where Malvolios too often rule households with disturbing propriety. The lovers have met, and Feste announces that present laughter has come to an end. But the actors, those true and untiring maskers, will continue to "strive to please" us. They will find few occasions in the future in which their efforts will be more sure of success.

Twelfth Night is the climax of Shakespeare's early achievement in comedy. The effects and values of the earlier comedies are here subtly embodied in the most complex structure which Shakespeare had yet created. But the play also looks forward: the pressure to dissolve the comedy, to realize and finally abandon the burden of laughter, is an intrinsic part of its "perfection." Viola's clear-eyed and affirmative vision of her own and the world's irrationality is a triumph and we desire it; yet we realize its vulnerability, and we come to realize that virtue in disguise is only totally triumphant when evil is not in disguise—virtue is not truly present at all. Having solved magnificently the problems of this particular form of comedy, Shakespeare was evidently not tempted to repeat his triumph. After *Twelfth Night* the so-called comedies require for their happy resolutions more radical characters and devices—omniscient and omnipresent Dukes, magic, and resurrection. More obvious miracles are needed for comedy to exist in a world in which evil also exists, not merely incipiently but with power.

The Design of *Twelfth Night*

by L. G. Salingar

Most readers of *Twelfth Night* would probably agree that this is
the most delightful, harmonious, and accomplished of Shakespeare's
romantic comedies, in many ways his crowning achievement in one
branch of his art. They would probably agree, too, that it has a
prevailing atmosphere of happiness, or at least of "tempests dissolved
in music." Yet there are striking differences of opinion over the design
of *Twelfth Night*. Is it, for example, a vindication of romance, or a
depreciation of romance?[1] Is it mainly a love story or a comedy of
humours; a "poem of escape" or a realistic comment on economic
security and prudential marriage?[2] And there are further variations.
The principal character, according to choice, is Viola, Olivia, Malvolio, or Feste.

To some extent, the play itself seems to invite such varying reac-
tions: *Twelfth Night; or, What You Will*. Shakespeare here is both
polishing his craftsmanship and exploring new facets of his experience,[3] so that the play has the buoyancy of a mind exhilarated by discovery, testing one human impulse against another, and satisfied with
a momentary state of balance which seems all the more trustworthy
because its limits have been felt and recognized. But in consequence,
Shakespeare's attitude towards his people comes near to humorous
detachment, to a kind of Socratic irony. He refrains from emphasizing

---

"*The Design of* Twelfth Night" *by L. G. Salingar. From the* Shakespeare Quarterly, *IX (1958), 117-139. Copyright © 1958 by the Shakespeare Association of America. Reprinted by permission of L. G. Salingar and the Shakespeare Association of
America. The essay has been slightly abridged for this volume.*

[1] Karl F. Thompson, "Shakespeare's Romantic Comedies," *PMLA*, LXVII (1952);
E. C. Pettet, *Shakespeare and the Romance Tradition* (1949), 122-132. "Tempests
dissolved in music" is the phrase of G. Wilson Knight, *The Shakespearian Tempest*
(1953 ed.), pp. 121-127.

[2] This is the interpretation of John W. Draper, *The Twelfth Night of Shakespeare's Audience* (Stanford Univ. Press, 1950).

[3] "Shakespearian comedy . . . speculates imaginatively on modes, not of preserving a good already reached, but of enlarging and extending the possibilities of
this and other kinds of good." H. B. Charlton, *Shakespearian Comedy* (1938), pp.
277-278.

any one of his themes at the expense of the rest. He carefully plays
down and transforms the crisis of sentiment in his main plot, while
giving unusual prominence to his comic subplot. He distributes the
interest more evenly among his characters than in *As You Like It* or
the other comedies, providing more numerous (and more unexpected)
points of contact between them, not only in the action but on the
plane of psychology. And the whole manner of *Twelfth Night* is light
and mercurial. The prose is full of ideas, but playful, not discursive.
The poetry, for all its lyrical glow, gives a sense of restraint and ease,
of keenly perceptive and yet relaxed enjoyment, rather than of any
compelling pressure of emotion.

Perhaps this attitude on Shakespeare's part is responsible for the
inconsistency of his interpreters. Those who dwell on the romantic
side of the play seem uncertain about its connection with the comic
realism; while those who concentrate on the elements of realism have
to meet the kind of objection gravely stated by Dr. Johnson—that "the
marriage of Olivia, and the succeeding perplexity, though well enough
contrived to divert on the stage, wants credibility, and fails to produce
the proper instruction required in the drama, as it exhibits no just
picture of life." The question to be interpreted, then, is how Shakespeare is using the instrument of theatrical contrivance, which is
present, of course, in all his comedies, but which he uses here with
exceptional delicacy and freedom.

Briefly, Shakespeare has taken a familiar kind of love story and
transformed it so as to extend the interest from the heroine to a
group of characters who reveal varying responses to the power of love.
He has modified the main situation further, and brought home his
comments on it, by using methods of construction he had mastered
previously in his *Comedy of Errors*. And he has added a subplot
based on the customary jokes and revels of a feast of misrule, when
normal restraints and relationships were overthrown. As the main
title implies, the idea of a time of misrule gives the underlying con-
structive principle of the whole play.

In *Twelfth Night*, as Miss Welsford puts it, Shakespeare "transmutes
into poetry the quintessence of the Saturnalia." [4] The subplot shows
a prolonged season of misrule, or "uncivil rule," in Olivia's household,

---

[4] Enid Welsford, *The Fool* (1935), p. 251; cp. E. K. Chambers, *Medieval Stage*
(1903), I, 403 n. Leslie Hotson gives further details connecting the play with the
Feast of Mis-rule in *The First Night of Twelfth Night* (1954), Ch. vii. To the
various possible meanings of Malvolio's yellow stockings (Hotson, p. 113) it is worth
adding that, according to Stubbes, yellow or green "or some other light wanton
colour" was the livery of "my Lord of Mis-rule" in the parishes (*Anatomy of Abuses*,
1583: ed. Furnivall, p. 147). Stubbes is speaking of summer games, but misrule was
not confined to Christmas—cp. *TN* (Arden edn.), III.iv.148: "More matter for a
May morning."

with Sir Toby turning night into day; there are drinking, dancing, and singing, scenes of mock wooing, a mock sword fight, and the gulling of an unpopular member of the household, with Feste mumming it as a priest and attempting a mock exorcism in the manner of the Feast of Fools. Sir Andrew and Malvolio resemble Ben Jonson's social pretenders;[5] but Shakespeare goes beyond Jonson in ringing the changes on the theme of Folly and in making his speakers turn logic and courtesy on their heads. A girl and a coward are given out to be ferocious duellists; a steward imagines that he can marry his lady; and finally a fool pretends to assure a wise man that darkness is light. In Feste, Shakespeare creates his most finished portrait of a professional fool; he is superfluous to the plot, but affects the mood of the play more than any other of Shakespeare's clowns.

Moreover, this saturnalian spirit invades the whole play. In the main plot, sister is mistaken for brother, and brother for sister. Viola tells Olivia "That you do think you are not what you are"—and admits that the same holds true of herself. The women take the initiative in wooing, both in appearance, and in fact; the heroine performs love-service for the lover. The Duke makes his servant "your master's mistress" and the lady who has withdrawn from the sight of men embraces a stranger. The four main actors all reverse their desires or break their vows before the comedy is over; while Antonio, the one single-minded representative of romantic devotion, is also the only character in the main plot who tries to establish a false identity and fails (III.iv.341-343); and he is left unrewarded and almost disregarded. Such reversals are, as Johnson says, devices peculiar to the stage, but Shakespeare makes them spring, or seem to spring, from the very nature of love. In the *Comedy of Errors* the confusions of identity are due to external circumstances; in *A Midsummer Night's Dream* Shakespeare begins to connect them with the capricious, illusory factor in subjective "fancy" that is common to the madman, the lover, and the creative poet. In *Twelfth Night,* he takes this similitude further. Love here will "be clamorous, and leap all civil bounds," like a lord of misrule; "love's night is noon," like Sir Toby's carousals. Love seems as powerful as the sea, tempestuous, indifferent, and changeable as the sea. And fortune, or fate, reveals the same paradoxical benevolence in this imbroglio of mistakes and disguises: "Tempests are kind, and salt waves fresh in love."

The analysis of love as a kind of folly was a common theme of Renaissance moralists, who delighted in contrasting it with the wisdom of the stoic or the man of affairs. Shakespeare's treatment of the theme

---

[5] P. Mueschke and J. Fleisher, "Jonsonian Elements in the Comic Underplot of *TN*," *PMLA*, XLVIII (1933).

in *Twelfth Night* is a natural development from his own previous work, but he could have found strong hints of it in the possible sources of his Viola-Orsino story. Bandello remarks, for instance, that it arouses wonder to hear of a gentleman disguising himself as a servant, and still more in the case of a girl: but when you realize that love is the cause, "the wonder ceases at once, because this passion of love is much too potent and causes actions much more amazing and excessive than that"; a person in love has "lost his liberty, and . . . no miracle if he commits a thousand errors." [6] And Barnabe Riche tells his readers that in his story of *Apolonius and Silla,* "you shall see Dame Error so play her part with a leash of lovers, a male and two females, as shall work a wonder to your wise judgment." [7] In effect, then, what Shakespeare could take for granted in his audience was not simply a readiness to be interested in romance, but a sense of the opposition between romance and reason.

On this basis, Shakespeare can unite his main action with his subplot, bending a romantic story in the direction of farce. By the same contrivances, he can disclose the follies surrounding love and celebrate its life-giving power. And he can do this, without sacrificing emotional reality—which is not exactly the same as Dr. Johnson's "just picture of life"—because he takes his stage machinery from the traditions of a

[6] "Ma come si dice che egli era innamorato, subito cessa l'ammirazione, perciò che questa passione amorosa è di troppo gran potere e fa far cose assai più meravigliose e strabocchevoli di questa. Né crediate che per altro la fabulosa Grecia finga i dèi innamorati aver fatte tante pazzie vituperose . . . , se non per darci ad intendere che come l'uomo si lascia soggiogar ad amore . . . , egli può dir d'aver giocata e perduta la sua libertà, e che miracolo non è se poi fa mille errori!" Bandello, *Le Novelle,* II, xxxvi (ed. G. Brognoligo [Bari: 1911], III, 252).

[7] Riche's *Apolonius and Silla* (ed. Morton Luce, *The Shakespeare Classics,* 1912), p. 53; cp. p. 52: "in all other things, wherein we show ourselves to be most drunken with this poisoned cup [of error], it is in our actions of love; for the lover is so estranged from that is right, and wandereth so wide from the bounds of reason, that he is not able to deem white from black . . . ; but only led by the appetite of his own affections, and grounding them on the foolishness of his own fancies, will so settle his liking on such a one, as either by desert or unworthiness will merit rather to be loathed than loved." Contrasts between love and reason are prominent, again, in Erasmus' *In Praise of Folly* and Sidney's *Arcadia,* two likely sources of the general themes of *TN.* Bacon's essay "Of Love" comes nearer still to the subject matter of Shakespeare's play, illustrating the tension of ideas there from a point of view almost directly opposite. "The stage is more beholding to love than the life of man; for as to the stage, love is ever matter of comedies, and now and then of tragedies; but in life it doth much mischief, sometimes like a Siren, sometimes like a Fury. . . . Great spirits and great business do keep out this weak passion . . . ; for whosoever esteemeth too much of amorous affection, quitteth both riches and wisdom. This passion hath his floods in the very times of weakness, which are, great prosperity and great adversity . . . ; both which times kindle love, and make it more fervent, and therefore show it to be the child of folly." This essay could almost be a commentary on Malvolio, Orsino, Viola, and Sebastian.

feast of misrule, where social custom has already begun to transform normal behavior into the material of comic art.[8] The whole play is a festivity, where reality and playacting meet. By presenting his main story on these lines, Shakespeare can develop his insight into the protean, contradictory nature of love with more economy and force than by keeping to the lines of an ordinary stage narrative. At the same time he can extend this theme through his realistic images of "uncivil rule" in the subplot, disclosing the conflicting impulses of an aristocratic community in a period of social change, and touching on the potentially tragic problems of the place of time and order in human affairs.

Shakespeare's intentions may stand out more clearly when one compares his treatment of the Viola story with its possible or probable sources.[9] The ultimate source is held to be the anonymous Sienese Comedy, *Gl'Ingannati* (*The Deceived*), first performed at a carnival of 1531 and frequently reprinted, translated, or imitated in the course of the sixteenth century. Shakespeare may also have known Bandello's story, which follows the plot of *Gl'Ingannati* closely, omitting the subordinate comic parts; and he probably knew Riche's *Apolonius*

---

[8] The idea of representing life as a festival of misrule was already implicit, of course, in the common notion that "all the world's a stage," and in the general Renaissance tradition of Folly, especially in Erasmus (cp. Welsford, pp. 236-242). Robert Armin, who acted Feste, may have helped to give point to the idea; in his *Nest of Ninnies* (1600-1608; ed. J. P. Collier, 1842), he represents the World, sick of a surfeit of drink and revelling, being shown a pageant of fools, who are partly endearing and partly symbols of the World's vices (cp. Welsford, pp. 162-165, 284). Armin does not treat of love, but John Heywood's *Play of Love* (-1533) is a Christmas interlude consisting of debates on the "reasons" of love between Lover not Loved, Loved not Loving (the woman), Lover Loved, and Neither Lover nor Loved (the Vice). And much nearer to *TN* comes Jonson's *Cynthia's Revels; or, the Fountain of Self-Love* (1600). Moreover, Shakespeare himself is very likely to have remembered the suggestive episode of December 28, 1594, when the *Comedy of Errors* was performed in the "disordered" revels of Gray's Inn: "So that Night was begun, and continued to the end, in nothing but Confusion and Errors; whereupon, it was ever afterwards called, *The Night of Errors*. . . . We preferred Judgments . . . against a Sorcerer or Conjuror that was supposed to be the cause of that confused Inconvenience . . . . And Lastly, that he had foisted a Company of base and common Fellows, to make up our Disorders with a Play of Errors and Confusions; and that that Night had gained to us Discredit, and itself a Nickname of Errors." (*Gesta Grayorum*; E. K. Chambers, *Shakespeare*, Appendix, "Performances"). Lastly, Shakespeare uses the metaphor of life as a mask of misrule directly in *Troilus*, a play linked in several ways with *TN:* "Degree being vizarded,/The unworthiest shows as fairly in the mask" (I.iii.83).

[9] This paragraph is based on Morton Luce's Arden ed. of *TN* (1906) and his ed. of Riche. Luce assembles parallels between *TN* and Riche, Bandello, and *Gl'Ingannati*, from which it seems very possible, though not certain, that Shakespeare knew any or all of the latter. Luce mentions, but does not examine, Shakespeare's debt to Plautus.

and Silla (1581), derived indirectly and with variations from Bandello. Another source of the main plot must have been the *Menaechmi* of Plautus, which presumably had already contributed something to *Gl'Ingannati*, but affects the composition of *Twelfth Night* more directly by way of *The Comedy of Errors*. In any case, Shakespeare's situations were part of the common stock of classical and medieval romance, as Manningham saw at one of the first performances of *Twelfth Night*, when he noted in his diary that it was "much like the Commedy of Errores, or Menechmi in Plautus, but most like and neere to that in Italian called *Inganni*" (one of the offshoots of *Gl'Ingannati*).

There are four essential characters common to *Gl'Ingannati*, Bandello, Riche, and Shakespeare; namely, a lover, a heroine in his service disguised as a page, her twin brother (who at first has disappeared), and a second heroine. The basic elements common to all four plots are: the heroine's secret love for her master; her employment as go-between, leading to the complication of a cross-wooing; and a final solution by means of the unforeseen arrival of the missing twin.

If Shakespeare knew Bandello or *Gl'Ingannati*, he altered their material radically. The Italians both take the romance motif of a heroine's constancy and love-service, set it in a realistic bourgeois environment, and rationalize it with respectful irony. In Bandello, the irony is severely rational—because it is a tale of love, "the wonder ceases at once." In *Gl'Ingannati*, the tone is whimsical. "Two lessons above all you will extract from this play," says the Prologue: "how much chance and good fortune can do in matters of love; and how much long patience is worth in such cases, accompanied by good advice." [10] Both Italian authors give the heroine a strong motive for assuming her disguise, in that the lover has previously returned her affection, but has now forgotten her and turned elsewhere. Both provide her with a formidable father in the background and a foster mother like Juliet's Nurse, who admonishes and helps her; and both credit her with the intention of bilking her rival if she can. On the other side, they both respect the code of courtly love to the extent of stressing the lover's penitence at the end, and his recognition that he must repay the heroine for her devotion. "I believe," he says in the play, "that this is certainly the will of God, who must have taken pity on this virtuous maiden and on my soul, that it should not go to perdition. . . ." [11]

---

[10] "Due ammaestramenti sopra tutto ne cavarete: quanto possa il caso e la buona fortuna nelle cose d'amore; e quanto, in quella, vaglia una longa pazienzia accompagnata da buon consiglio" (ed. I. Sanesi, *Commedie del Cinquecento*, Bari, 1912, I, 316).

[11] "Io credo che questa sia certamente volontá di Dio che abbia avuto pietá di

Riche keeps this framework of sentiment, vulgarizes the narrative, and changes some of the material circumstances, generally in the direction of an Arcadian romance.

Shakespeare, for his part, changes the story fundamentally, broadening the interest and at the same time making the whole situation more romantically improbable, more melancholy at some points, more fantastic at others. He stiffens the heroine's loyalty, but deprives her of her original motive, her initiative, and her family. In place of these, he gives her the background of a vague "Messaline" and a romantic shipwreck, for which he may have taken a hint, but no more, from the episode of the shipwreck in Riche. Shakespeare's Viola, then, is a more romantic heroine than the rest, and the only one to fall in love *after* assuming her disguise. At the same time, however, Shakespeare enlarges the role of her twin brother and gives unprecedented weight to coincidence in the denouement, which in both Italian stories is brought about more rationally, by the deliberate action of the heroine and her nurse; so that Shakespeare's Viola is also unique in that her happiness is due to "good fortune" more than "long patience," and to "good advice" not at all.

In his exposition, therefore, Shakespeare sketches a situation from romance in place of a logical intrigue. But the purpose, or at any rate, the effect, of his plan is to shift attention at the outset from the circumstances of the love story to the sentiments as such, especially in their more mysterious and irrational aspects. Shakespeare may have taken hints, for Orsino and Olivia, from his predecessors' comments on the "error" of "following them that fly from us." But however that may be, his comedy now consists in the triumph of natural love over affectation and melancholy. And, taken together, the leading characters in *Twelfth Night* form the most subtle portrayal of the psychology of love that Shakespeare had yet drawn. . . .

---

questa virtuosa giovane e dell'anima mia; ch'ella non vada in perdizione. E però, madonna Lelia, . . . io non voglio altra moglie che voi . . ." (V,iii; ed. Sanesi, p. 393). Cp. Bandello, pp. 273-275; Riche, p. 82.

Mistakes in *Twelfth Night* and Their Resolution: A Study in Some Relationships of Plot and Theme

by Porter Williams, Jr.

A study of the significance of the mistakes in *Twelfth Night,* like the study of any important aspect of Shakespeare's art, must be made upon several levels, for mistakes by the protagonists are both a part of the superficial fabric of the plot and a subtle means of revealing underlying themes that often manifest themselves only indirectly below the surface action. This is not to say that the artificial devices of disguises and mistaken identities, all timeworn devices, are nothing more than a mere plot framework for the profundities that lie beneath. Rather, as Miss Bradbrook expresses it, there is an "interdependence of the natural and the artificial, the human and the literary." [1] The ridiculous mistakes that control the plot are therefore like Freudian slips which incite their superficial laughter and at the same time reveal subconscious patterns of human behavior. It is these slips, the mistakes of all the leading characters, that we must follow into the thematic material of the play, for it is on this level that they become of most interest.

Twelfth Night, then, on its superficial level is based upon familiar patterns, suggesting Plautus and Italian Renaissance comedy. Characters are symmetrically grouped, there are disguises, a twin brother and sister, a fool, and scarcely believable deceptions.[2] Added to this is something of the comic spirit of the Twelfth Night Feast of the Epiphany in which the world is turned topsy-turvy. Traditionally in such celebrations, servants change places with their masters and say

[1] M. C. Bradbrook, *Shakespeare and Elizabethan Poetry* (London, 1951), p. 228.
[2] M. C. Bradbrook, *The Growth and Structure of Elizabethan Comedy* (London, 1955), pp. 78, 86.

what they please, jests and pranks may be carried out with impunity, and the Fool becomes enthroned as the Lord of Misrule.[3] All of this Italian artificiality and the happy Twelfth Night nonsense can be felt as a background in Shakespeare's play, though they have been transformed into something that is sophisticated and even profound, possibly designed for a learned audience at the Inns of Court or to be acted before the Queen, as Leslie Hotson would have it.[4] Thus the maskings, deceptions, and the foolery may suggest the celebrations of the traditional Masks and Revels, or even hint at the seriousness behind such religious holidays, but they have been "translated into an entirely different idiom." [5] Nevertheless, disguises and deceptions of one sort or another dominate the play, and the errors to be studied spring from them. These disguises may be merely physical, as with Viola dressed as a page or Feste dressed as Sir Topas, or they may be psychological, as with Orsino and Olivia who have deceived themselves into believing that they have been overwhelmed with love or with grief. Such disguises may fool others or only the deceiver. Out of this emerges the full richness of one of Shakespeare's finest romantic comedies.

Superficially, the plot may be seen to develop in terms of Exposition, Complication, and Resolution, which might be described as masking, the resulting deceptions and errors, and a final unmasking. But the significant developments and revelations of character, and even the resolution of the errors, take place beneath this sparkling surface of disguises. The play opens to reveal Orsino and Olivia at an impasse, and both wear psychological masks, for one is foolishly determined to renounce love and grieve seven years for the loss of a brother; while the other, overcome with love melancholy, is determined that he can love only the woman who rejects him. Orsino's melancholy is reminiscent of the sadness that lengthens Romeo's hours while he is away from his unresponsive Rosaline. These are the two great mistakes opening the play, for Olivia and Orsino are self-deceived, both assuming false personalities and unaware that by all the rules of romantic comedy and love psychology, they are destined for marriage, though not to each other. The Complication of the play begins with the entrance of Viola disguised as the page Cesario, the central deception of the play; and the action of the main plot as well as of the subplots may be

[3] Leslie Hotson, *The First Night of Twelfth Night* (London, 1954), pp. 97-99. See also Sir E. K. Chambers, *The Mediaeval Stage* (Oxford, 1903), on Epiphany customs and the Feast of Fools.

[4] Sir E. K. Chambers, *William Shakespeare* (Oxford, 1930), I, 405, and Hotson, *The First Night of Twelfth Night*.

[5] Bradbrook, *Shakespeare and Elizabethan Poetry*, p. 230.

said to proceed as a series of thwarted suits for the hand of Olivia or the love of Orsino. Mistakes control the direction of action throughout. Viola cannot obtain Orsino's love as long as she is mistaken for Cesario and as long as Orsino mistakes the object of his love; while Olivia, though abandoning one error, that of a seven years' grief, still cannot love Orsino and can never win the disguised Viola. Olivia's other suitors, Sir Andrew Aguecheek and Malvolio, hopelessly deceived into playing the roles of lovers, are fooled each to the top of his bent until unmasked before all by Sir Toby, Maria, and their associates in the subplot. The action reaches its turning point with the cleverest "disguise" of all and the happiest deception. Sebastian, appearing as himself and hence unwittingly disguised as Cesario, his masked sister, accepts the hand of Olivia, now most truly herself and yet most completely deceived. Only unmasking can follow after this, with the pairing off of the lovers and the dismissal of the thwarted. Feste, the wisest fool of them all, is left alone to frame the action in Time.

It has already been suggested that mistakes, besides being at the center of the superficial and hardly believable fabric of disguises and deceptions that activate the plot, are also at the center of the rich psychological revelations that represent the important themes of the play and supply a believable kind of motivation. Errors on this level supply startling insights into patterns that run through many of Shakespeare's plays. On this level, deceptions, or the effort to deceive, and the mistakes they produce, all tend to reveal rather than to hide human nature. There is a danger here, of course, of losing sight of the specific problem of mistakes by merely repeating what has already been discussed so admirably by such critics as Professor H. B. Charlton, Miss M. C. Bradbrook, and Professor J. R. Brown. In a sense most of the themes that are implicit in all of Shakespeare's comedies cross the pattern of mistakes in *Twelfth Night*. Our problem here will be to show not so much that the comedies are informed by Shakespeare's "attitude to life and, in particular, to love and personal relationships," [6] but to show that the mistakes themselves have an intimate bearing upon the revelation of these themes of love and personal relationships. It is through his mistakes that we can see a character in the play either find or avoid what for him is a right relationship. For example, Olivia's spontaneous love for Cesario, a mistake on most levels, unconsciously prepares her heart for a happy union with Sebastian, just as it also reveals the fallacy of contemplating an unnatural seven years' grief. Likewise, Sebastian, thrust into a world of misconceptions but sensing his own occasion mellow, accepts an offer of marriage in complete

[6] John Russell Brown, *Shakespeare and His Comedies* (London, 1957), p. 160.

ignorance and fully aware only "That this may be some error"
(IV.iii.10).[7]

The examples above lead naturally to a control point for a discussion
of mistakes—the marriage of Olivia and Sebastian, the happiest and
most important error in the play. Superficially, it is a daring and spontaneous act, suggestive even of the "too rash, too unadvis'd, too
sudden" betrothal in *Romeo and Juliet* (II.ii.118). Olivia is aware of
her haste and anxiety:

> Plight me the full assurance of your faith,
> That my most jealous and too doubtful soul
> May live at peace.   (IV.iii.26-28)

Likewise, Sebastian is enwrapped in "wonder," aware of the possibility of "error" or even "madness," and ready to "distrust" his eyes
and "wrangle" with his reason (IV.iii.1-21). And yet these mistakes
are fortunate ones of the mind rather than the heart, even though
Olivia thinks that she is marrying Cesario. Intuition, not reason, is
at work. Unlike Malvolio, they find happiness because they know what
it is "To be generous, guiltless, and of free disposition" (I.v.89-90).
Such impulses can bring tragic disaster, especially if fiery Tybalts or
jealous Iagos are about; but given a world this side of tragedy, then
the generous impulses of open natures are the surest way to happiness. A willingness to love and, something more, perhaps the gift to
recognize a kindred spirit and to risk all, are the touchstones to
Shakespeare's serious world of romantic comedy. Olivia's words, "Love
sought is good . . . but given unsought is better" (III.i.158), seem to
be the dominant note for those who win happiness in terms of love
and friendship, but such giving and receiving must be done without
counting the cost or measuring the risk. Viola gives her love unsought to Orsino, while on a more material level a surprising quantity
of money and rings is given generously throughout the play, sought and
unsought. Viola awards the Sea Captain gold without being asked, and
she is quite willing to share what she has with the perplexed Antonio.
Antonio gives unasked to Sebastian, and all pour coins into the open
hand of the Fool.[8] Seldom in a play does money flow so freely or so
readily to symbolize generous love and friendship. Olivia specializes
in sending rings and pearls to those she loves, though not quite so
spontaneously as to be unaware that "youth is bought more oft than
begged or borrowed" (III.iv.3); and even the irritable Orsino sends to

[7] All references to *Twelfth Night* are from *The New Shakespeare,* ed. Sir Arthur
Quiller-Couch and John Dover Wilson (Cambridge, 1949).

[8] See I.ii.17; I.v.305; II.iii.28; II.iv.67; III.i.43ff.; III.iii.38ff.; III.iv.343; IV.i.18;
IV.iii.2; V.i.27ff.

inform his "sovereign cruelty" that neither her "quantity of dirty lands" nor her fortune interests him,

> But 'tis that miracle and queen of gems
> That nature pranks her in attracts my soul.
>
> (II.iv.85-86)

Perhaps his love should have gone deeper than the "gem" of her beauty, though surely the note of generosity is there. In sharp contrast to these generous lovers is Malvolio, who is rebuked by Olivia for being neither "generous" nor "free" (I.v.89-90), not to mention Sir Toby's obvious abuse of friendship in his typical reminder to Sir Andrew that "Thou hadst need send for more money," or Sir Andrew's equally mercenary reply, "If I cannot recover your niece, I am a foul way out" (II.iii.189-190). Shakespeare makes it clear enough that such self-love and mercenary friendship lead nowhere, for all three are used according to their desert. These are their mistakes. The secret of true love and friendship, therefore, is a subtle and delicate relationship, depending upon uncalculating generosity and spontaneous impulses. Professor H. B. Charlton links this idea to the Elizabethan discovery that man was "a much less rational and a much more complex creature than he had taken himself to be." More than this, man had discovered that his instincts, intuitions, and emotions were "often a much more exciting and satisfying part of his nature than was his sober intellect." For the express purpose of comedy, man was becoming intellectually aware that "the tumultuous condition of his being which followed his falling in love and urged him on to woo, was in fact no mean and mainly physical manifestation of his personality; it was, in fact, the awakening in him of the fuller capacities of his spirit." [9] Shakespeare was particularly adept at underlying the awakening of these spiritual capacities by revealing them while the reason was perplexed with error, with the very mistakes that threatened well laid plans opening the way for intuitive solutions. Olivia's marriage to Sebastian, a farcical mistake of her intellect, nevertheless allows Shakespeare to explore with sympathy "the subtle flow of unacknowledged attraction between man and woman." [10] The very tone of the poetry conveys the spiritual quality of Olivia's "most extracting frenzy" as she goes with Sebastian to the priest who is to marry them:

> Then lead the way, good father, and heavens so shine,
> That they may fairly note this act of mine!
>
> (IV.iii.34-35)

[9] H. B. Charlton, *Shakespearian Comedy* (London, 1949), p. 281.
[10] Bradbrook, *The Growth and Structure of Elizabethan Comedy,* p. 92.

Sebastian also takes his "fair hour" with equal rapture. The verse alone
informs us that all is well:

> This is the air, that is the glorious sun,
> This pearl she gave me, I do feel't and see't,
> And though 'tis wonder that enwraps me thus,
> Yet 'tis not madness.   (IV.iii.1-4)

Add to this the solemn words of the priest as he mistakenly testifies to
having performed the holy ceremony of wedlock between Olivia and
Cesario, and we see the richest fulfillment of spiritual capacities under
the surface of error. With the thoughts of the jealous Duke ripe in
mischief, the Priest announces

> A contract of eternal bond of love,
> Confirmed by mutual joinder of your hands,
> Attested by the holy close of lips,
> Strength'ned by interchangement of your rings,
> And all the ceremony of this compact
> Sealed in my function, by my testimony:
>
> (V.i.155-160)

The Priest's confusion, even if it should be a moment for laughter, is
also the final blessing of the marriage of Olivia and Sebastian. Unmasking after this can only reveal what has already been fulfilled under the "darkness" of error.

Further light can be thrown on the subtle flow of attraction between
man and woman by examining some of the unhappy errors in the play,
the errors of the unsuccessful suitors. These errors reveal no redeeming
capacities of the spirit. Malvolio's "rapture" has nothing to do with
love, and Sir Andrew's hopes draw on nothing more than the recollection that he "was adored once too" (II.iii.188). Malvolio loves only
the selfish vision of "Count Malvolio" with all the coveted trappings
of officers, velvet gowns, rich jewels, and the "prerogative of speech"
(II.v.24ff.). He would like to think that Olivia "did affect" him, but
there is no underlying love to redeem his error of exposing to the
world his impossible ambition of becoming Count Malvolio:

> I will be proud, I will read politic authors, I will baffle Sir Toby, I will
> wash off gross acquaintance, I will be point-devise the very man. I do
> not now fool myself, to let imagination jade me; for every reason excites
> to this, that my lady loves me.
>
> (II.v.165-169)

This selfish dream was too large for a mere steward and could not
stand the test of reality. Once he had imagined his dream to be real,
the real world took its harsh revenge. Similarly, Sir Andrew came to

grief by trying to rise to the dignified role of knighthood. Deceived
into believing that he was loved, he made a fool of himself as he
bought Sir Toby's friendship and bargained for a fortune. He leaves
the stage fleeced and unloved, redeemed by no spiritual capacities, and
content once again to be Sir Toby's drinking companion.

Orsino, a more dignified suitor, presents the same kind of com-
plexities as Olivia. Like Olivia, he too had a spirit capable of being
awakened, but like her he made the mistake of assuming a false mask,
that of a self-centered melancholy delighting in the luxurious inac-
tivity of unrequited love. His finer nature is so mesmerized by self-
indulgence that he almost forgets to seek the object of his love except
in the dream world of rich music. "Instead of seeking opportunities
to 'give and hazard,' he passively takes what seeming pleasures can be
his." [11] This is his mistake, and like Olivia he must be tricked into
awakening by another's fresh, spontaneous love. This is the work of
Viola.

Viola, both protagonist and catalyst in the central action of the
play, suffers and triumphs through the mistakes of others. She too must
take part in masking and deceit, and yet she is the least deceived of
the three. Her mask is a physical disguise and not one of the spirit, for
she knows herself always to be "one heart, one bosom and one truth"
(III.i.160). Her mistakes rise out of her inability to foresee all of the
consequences of her disguising, not from any self-deceit, but this is
enough to bring her close to disaster and to force her to respond with
all the chords of her rich personality. Her first unexpected difficulty
arises when she finds that in the role of Cesario she must against her
own good unfold the passion of Orsino's love to Olivia, a task she
undertakes so honorably that she ends by charming Olivia and winning
her love. Already she has discovered the unexpected complications that
can arise from deceit, however good one's intentions:

> Disguise, I see thou art a wickedness,
> Wherein the pregnant enemy does much.
> (II.ii.27-28)

Consequently she must continue to throw herself upon the mercy of
time and the unknown:

> O time, thou must untangle this, not I,
> It is too hard a knot for me t'untie.
> (II.ii.40-41)

Other complications follow that draw heavily upon her reserves, for
as Cesario she must face the unexpected "rivalry" of Sir Andrew and

[11] Brown, p. 164.

the jealous rage of her own master, Duke Orsino. The first exposes her to a test of her courage and to ridicule, as well as to the accusations of ingratitude from Antonio; the second brings her close to death. She learns how truly difficult it is to pretend to be a man:

> Pray God defend me! A little thing would
> make me tell them how much I lack of a man.
>
> (III.iv.300-301)

But left to the care of time, Viola's mistakes or miscalculations operate to clarify the mistakes of others. Her "one heart" and her "one truth" secretly bring about the resolution of all her problems, for she is not deceived about the essentials of love. In spite of her own difficulties, all the great mistakes of the play can be evaluated against her "one truth." This can best be seen by discussing her complex relationships to Orsino and Olivia.

In the very first scene of *Twelfth Night* we are presented with the two great mistakes of Orsino's lovesickness and Olivia's unnatural effort to "keep fresh/And lasting, in her sad remembrance" all the wealth of a "brother's dead love" (I.i.30-31). Orsino unwittingly touches upon Olivia's mistake when he comments upon this "debt of love but to a brother" and anticipates the wealth of love in her nature which she is trying to deny:

> How will she love, when the rich golden shaft
> Hath killed the flock of all affections else
> That live in her . . .   (I.i.34-36)

Olivia has yet to learn, in the words of the Fool, that "beauty's a flower" subject to time (I.v.50), and in the words of Viola, that "what is yours to bestow, is not yours to reserve" (I.v.189). Here, again, is the Duke willing to console himself with music for seven inactive years, and a Countess willing to stifle her rich wealth of love for the same length of time in useless grief. A few lines later, in dramatic contrast to the themes of frustration and wasted time of the opening scene, Viola presents her first rich "commentary" upon Olivia and Orsino. She too has lost a brother and feels the apathy of true grief: "And what should I do in Illyria?" (I.ii.3) Then quite spontaneously she thinks of her brother as happy in "Elysium," though at the same time is still willing to hope that "Perchance he is not drowned" (I.ii.5). Like her brother, "Courage and hope both teaching him the practice" (I.ii.13), she will make the best of what life offers: "Mine own escape unfoldeth to my hope" (I.ii.18). This hope unfolds itself with startling swiftness at the mention of Orsino's name and the words: "He was a bachelor then!" No bachelor duke is safe against a mind of this swiftness, however long the time to untangle events between the thought and the "occasion mellow." A final commentary on Viola's willingness to trust herself to time and to the responsive goodness in others can be found in her words to the Captain:

> There is a fair behaviour in thee, captain,
> And though that nature with a beauteous wall
> Doth oft close in pollution, yet of thee
> I will believe thou hast a mind that suits
> With this thy fair and outward character.   (I.ii.46-50)

Viola's free and generous nature, though perhaps incautious, is not a sign of naïve inexperience. As will be shown later, she well knows that "wickedness" can appear in "disguise" (II.ii.27), but she instinctively realizes that fulfillment of inner promise involves commitment to events:

> What else may hap to time I will commit,
> Only shape thou thy silence to my wit.
>   (I.ii.59-60)

The errors of Olivia and Orsino stand sharply revealed here. In terms of the fulfillment of love's wealth, "In delay there lies no plenty" (II.iii.52).

Once Viola enters the stage as Cesario, fully involved in the action herself, she continues to offer her "commentary" upon the error of denying love's fulfillment. Like Rosalind in *As You Like It,* she teaches others the true meaning of love—the kind of love that would bring a woman down upon her knees to "thank heaven, fasting, for a good man's love" (*As You Like It,* III.v.57-58). Phebe and Orlando profit from such instruction, as do Olivia and Orsino, though Viola's subtle lessons must thread their way through more complex obstacles. But the instruction is persuasive, for the teacher speaks from her own heart, and error itself helps point the way to truth. Olivia abandons the error of seeking a "brother's dead love" only to mistake Viola as an object of her new love. But this mistake, though perhaps begun by her being charmed with Cesario's fair "outside" (II.ii.18), soon leads to an intensity of love that is far deeper than the pain of Orsino's "Unstaid and skittish" love (II.iv.18). Nevertheless, the error of being mistaken in the object of her love bears for Olivia its own rich reward, for it has prepared her to love Sebastian at first sight. We have here an interesting variation of the Platonic doctrine of "elective affinity," for we see Olivia fall in love with Viola and then Sebastian at first sight, while at the same time we can also say that the mistake of loving Viola has really prepared Olivia for giving herself generously to Sebastian. In this sense, she loves Sebastian before seeing him because she has learned to love him through Viola. The psychology here is perhaps sounder

than that of the lover in Donne's "The Good-Morrow" who excuses
his past conquests as a mere preparation:

> If ever any beauty I did see,
> Which I desir'd, and got, 'twas but a dream of thee.

Viola stood for something much more substantial than a mere dream
of Sebastian, and the consequent marriage by mistake to Sebastian
needs no apology. Similarly Orsino, not really profoundly in love with
Olivia, learns in his subtle relationship with his page Cesario something of the depth of true love, and is therefore prepared through that
aspect of Viola hidden in Cesario to accept the real Viola the instant
she is unmasked. More than one meaning is revealed in Viola's beauti-
ful lines,

> I am all the daughters of my father's house,
> And all the brothers too . . . .   (II.iv.120-121)

Among other meanings, at this point in her relationships to both Orsino and Olivia, she is creating as one person subtle ties that will become binding for her brother as well as for herself. It is the denouement that must unmask Viola, reveal a brother and sister, and pair off
lovers already destined for each other. The unmasked Viola will be no
stranger to Orsino, nor Sebastian to Olivia. Like the sudden conver-
sion of Beatrice and Benedict in *Much Ado About Nothing*, the apparently superficial and hasty avowal of love has had its stormy preparation in misunderstanding.

Above everything else, it is Viola's love for Orsino that secretly
teaches both Olivia and Orsino the true meaning of love and emphasizes the ridiculous inadequacies of Malvolio, Sir Andrew, and even
the affectionate Sir Toby. Viola's love may have been disguised; it
could not be entirely hid. In sharp contrast is the introspective Duke,
eloquent as he compares the constancy of his own love to that of a
woman's, but he is not speaking from experience:

> There is no woman's sides
> Can bide the beating of so strong a passion
> As love doth give my heart: no woman's heart
> So big, to hold so much, they lack retention.
> Alas, their love may be called appetite—
> No motion of the liver, but the palate—
> That suffers surfeit, cloyment and revolt;
> But mine is all as hungry as the sea,
> And can digest as much. Make no compare
> Between that love a woman can bear me
> And that I owe Olivia.   (II.iv.93-103)

The Duke is wrong; and Viola's answer, based upon her own intense passion, is one that gives "a very echo to the seat/Where Love is throned" (II.iv.21-22). Viola knows only too well "what love women to men may owe" (II.iv.105). Here she tells her own sad story to counter the Duke's argument:

> My father had a daughter loved a man,
> As it might be, perhaps, were I a woman,
> I should your lordship.   (II.iv.107-109)

Unlike Olivia, only too well does she know the danger of wasting time by sitting "like Patience on a monument,/Smiling at grief" (II.iv.114-115). This danger has been made all the more intense by the unconscious cruelty of the Duke's earlier reference to time:

> For women are as roses, whose fair flower
> Being once displayed doth fall that very hour.
>   (II.iv.38-39)

Knowing her own constancy, she can at least risk telling the Duke some of the things about love that he does not yet know:

> We men may say more, swear more—but indeed
> Our shows are more than will; for still we prove
> Much in our vows, but little in our love.
>   (II.iv.116-118)

Not until the last scene of the play does Orsino experience the full truth in this, when he reveals his own divided heart and threatens to kill, "had I the heart to do it," both Olivia and Viola. His language here betrays his own shifting devotion, for he first threatens Olivia with the words, "Why should I not . . . Kill what I love" (V.i.116-118); and then he turns upon Viola, threatening her also, but at the same time using terms of affection that seem to warm into love:

> But this your minion [Cesario], whom I know you love,
> And whom, by heaven I swear, I tender dearly,
> Him will I tear out of that cruel eye   (V.i.124-126)

Three lines later he is saying, "I'll sacrifice the lamb *that I do love.*" And shortly after this when Viola is unmasked, of course, the Duke is fully prepared to call Viola "Orsino's mistress and his fancy's queen" (V.i.387). At last he finds his right love, but surely not through the kind of constancy of which he had bragged. Such constancy was Viola's alone, and there is no more moving proof of this than the moment at which Viola turns to follow the angry Duke to her own sacrifice:

> And I, most jocund, apt and willingly,
> To do you rest, a thousand deaths would die.
>
> (V.i.131-132)

Comedy here touches for a fleeting moment the pathos of tragedy. Viola's love would have endured a test as final as Desdemona's.

Olivia, too, receives her painful lessons about love from Viola. For example, Viola adopts the tone of the *Sonnets* in what comes close to being the kind of rebuke a Rosalind might have given in a courtly setting:

> Lady, you are the cruell'st she alive,
> If you will lead these graces to the grave,
> And leave the world no copy.   (I.v.245-247)

Later, Viola perhaps has herself in mind when she tells Olivia how she would love if she were Orsino:

> Make me a willow cabin at your gate.
> And call upon my soul within the house,
> Write loyal cantons of contemned love,
> And sing them loud even in the dead of night
>
> (I.v.272-275)

This almost parodies the language of an outworn code of love, but a fresh sincerity is in the speaker. Viola, to her surprise, reaps an unexpected reward for her sincere efforts when she undertakes Orsino's commission and finds herself beloved of Olivia. This is perhaps Viola's greatest error, but it serves to teach Olivia all she needs to know about herself and her waste of time, though more than once Viola must remind her "That you do think you are not what you are" (III.i.141). Such, then, are the deceptions and self-deceptions of Olivia and Orsino. It takes the love of Viola, knowing herself and trusting to time, to untangle the web of mistakes.

No one in *Twelfth Night* entirely escapes the darkness of ignorance, but at least those who come to know generous love and friendship escape time's harshest revenges. Those who escape make it clear why the others suffered, for comedy thrives on poetic justice. Viola is always the touchstone, though Feste may point the moral. Once Viola emerges from the sea, displays her courage and hope, and reveals her generous capacity for love, we have our standard by which to judge the others. Thus Sebastian reaps his fine reward by following his sister's path of openhearted commitment to events. We can expect Antonio, the model of generous friendship, to find generosity in return, as will the Captain who helped Viola, though mistakes have been obstacles to them. Interestingly enough, some of the most important statements about friendship and generosity are made each time Viola and Antonio meet and quarrel over the vice of ingratitude. Either Viola or Antonio might have been given the following words as they confronted each other:

> I hate ingratitude more in a man,
> Than lying vainness, babbling drunkenness,
> Or any taint of vice whose strong corruption
> Inhabits our frail blood. (III.iv.352-355)

The words are Viola's, addressed to Antonio who has mistaken her for an ungrateful Sebastian. Neither of them is tainted with any of the vices listed in the passage, but the list may easily be related to the errors that lead the minor characters into the den of error. Malvolio's vanity, Sir Toby's drunkenness and unkindness, and Sir Andrew's foolish limitations, all show how far short they fall in human relationships.

In terms of the action of the drama, it is the appearance of Sebastian and Viola together that is the signal for the final resolution of all mistakes, although in another sense the appearance of Sebastian is merely a revelation of what has already been resolved earlier on a hidden level. The Duke's startled comment upon seeing Viola and Sebastian together for the first time makes clear to all that most of the problems have already been solved: "One face, one voice, one habit, and *two* persons" (V.i.215). In short, Olivia's mistaken marriage has already given her the right husband, and Orsino's unconscious love for Cesario has made it clear where he is to find an adoring wife. Antonio and the kind Captain need now fear no breach in true friendship. And Viola finds a brother whose presence she has already half suspected and a husband she already loves. As for the injured parties, they come to see the cause of their miseries, their own foolish errors. Sir Andrew experiences the limitations of a shallow friendship, Malvolio the end of an egotistical dream, and Sir Toby the end of at least one foolish jest and his irresponsible bachelorhood. Virtue, openheartedness, and sense have prevailed, although no one has escaped the perplexities of mistakes, and no one has escaped being called a fool or mad. As the wisest of fools observes, "Foolery, sir, does walk about the orb like the sun, it shines every where" (III.i.38-40).

The wise and the generous, then, survive their foolish mistakes, and profit. Most important of all, there has been revealed a kind of wisdom of the heart that flourishes even while the intellect is perplexed. Feste's remark that "there is no darkness but ignorance" (IV.ii.42-43) achieves its fullest meaning on this deeper spiritual or psychological level. It is strange that a study of mistakes, instead of restricting criticism to a discussion of superficial farce, leads directly to the inner life of the play. Every mistake may be a blemish of the mind, but the inner life of the play reveals that only the blemishes of the heart destroy:

> In nature there's no blemish but the mind;
> None can be called deformed but the unkind.
>   (III.iv.365-366)

This is a note running through all of Shakespeare.

Beyond this point lie the tragedies, exploring again the problems of the heart, but presenting monstrous deformities and disastrous mistakes. In this darker world, death would have entered to measure the depth of Viola's love. It is enough for the world of the comedies that *Twelfth Night* closes with Feste's cryptic song after the happy talk of marriage to remind us once again of time, mortality, and the passing of all things—a tragic theme that scarcely disturbs between the "curtain" and the applause.

Liberty Testing Courtesy

by C. L. Barber

We have seen how each of the festive comedies tends to focus on a particular kind of folly that is released along with love—witty masquerade in *Love's Labour's Lost*, delusive fantasy in *A Midsummer Night's Dream*, romance in *As You Like It*, and, in *The Merchant of Venice*, prodigality balanced against usury. *Twelfth Night* deals with the sort of folly which the title points to, the folly of misrule. But the holiday reference limits its subject too narrowly: the play exhibits the liberties which gentlemen take with decorum in the pursuit of pleasure and love, including the liberty of holiday, but not only that. Such liberty is balanced against timeserving. As Bassanio's folly of prodigality leads in the end to gracious fulfillment, so does Viola's folly of disguise. There is just a suggestion of the risks when she exclaims, not very solemnly,

> Disguise, I see thou art a wickedness
> Wherein the pregnant enemy does much (II.ii.28-29)

As in *The Merchant of Venice* the story of a prodigal is the occasion for an exploration of the use and abuse of wealth, so here we get an exhibition of the use and abuse of social liberty.

What enables Viola to bring off her role in disguise is her perfect courtesy, in the large, humanistic meaning of that term as the Renaissance used it, the *corteziania* of Castiglione. Her mastery of courtesy goes with her being the daughter of "that Sebastian of Messalina whom I know you have heard of": gentility shows through her disguise as does the fact that she is a woman. The impact on Olivia of Cesario's quality as a gentleman is what is emphasized as the countess, recalling their conversation, discovers that she is falling in love:

> 'What is thy parentage?'
> 'Above my fortunes, yet my state is well.

"Liberty Testing Courtesy" by C. L. Barber. From Ch. 10, "Testing Courtesy and Humanity in Twelfth Night," in Shakespeare's Festive Comedy (Princeton, N.J.: Princeton University Press, 1959), pp. 248-57. Copyright © 1959 by the Princeton University Press. Reprinted by permission of the publisher.

> I am a gentleman.' I'll be sworn thou art.
> Thy tongue, thy face, thy limbs, actions, and spirit
> Do give thee fivefold blazon. Not too fast! soft, soft!
> Unless the master were the man.   (I.v.308-313)

We think of manners as a mere prerequisite of living decently, like cleanliness. For the Renaissance, they could be almost the end of life, as the literature of courtesy testifies. *Twelfth Night* carries further an interest in the fashioning of a courtier which, as Miss Bradbrook points out,[1] appears in several of the early comedies, especially *The Two Gentlemen of Verona*, and which in different keys Shakespeare was pursuing, about the same time as he wrote *Twelfth Night*, in *Hamlet* and *Measure for Measure*. People in *Twelfth Night* talk of courtesy and manners constantly. But the most important expression of courtesy of course is in object lessons. It is their lack of breeding and manners which makes the comic butts ridiculous, along with their lack of the basic, free humanity which, be it virile or feminine, is at the center of courtesy and flowers through it.

Mr. Van Doren, in a fine essay, observes that *Twelfth Night* has a structure like *The Merchant of Venice*. "Once again Shakespeare has built a world out of music and melancholy, and once again this world is threatened by an alien voice. The opposition of Malvolio to Orsino and his class parallels the opposition of Shylock to Antonio and his friends. The parallel is not precise, and the contrast is more subtly contrived; Shakespeare holds the balance in a more delicate hand. . . ."[2] One way in which this more delicate balance appears is that the contest of revellers with intruder does not lead to neglecting ironies about those who are on the side of pleasure. We are all against Malvolio, certainly, in the great moment when the whole opposition comes into focus with Toby's "Dost thou think, because thou art virtuous, there shall be no more cakes and ale?" (II.iii.123-125) The festive spirit shows up the killjoy vanity of Malvolio's decorum. The steward shows his limits when he calls misrule "this uncivil rule." But one of the revellers is Sir Andrew, who reminds us that there is no necessary salvation in being a fellow who delights "in masques and revels sometimes altogether" (I.iii.121). There was no such ninny pleasure-seeker in *The Merchant of Venice*; his role continues Shallow's, the would-be reveller who is comically inadequate. To put such a leg as his into "a flame-coloured stock" only shows how meager it is. This thin creature's motive is self-improvement: he is a version of the stock type of prodigal who is gulled in trying to learn how to be gallant. As in Restoration comedy the fop confirms the values of the rake, Aguecheek serves as

[1] *Shakespeare and Elizabethan Poetry,* Ch. IX.
[2] *Shakespeare,* p. 161.

foil to Sir Toby. But he also marks one limit as to what revelry can do for a man: "I would I had bestowed that time in the tongues that I have in fencing, dancing and bearbaiting" (I.iii.97-99).

Sir Toby is gentlemanly liberty incarnate, a specialist in it. He lives at his ease, enjoying heritage, the something-for-nothing which this play celebrates, as *The Merchant of Venice* celebrates wealth—what he has without having to deserve it is his kinsman's place in Olivia's household:

> *Maria.* What a caterwauling do you keep here! If my lady have not call'd up her steward Malvolio and bid him turn you out of doors, never trust me.
>
> *Sir Toby.* My lady's a Catayan, we are politicians, Malvolio's a Peg-a-Ramsay, and [sings] "Three merry men be we." Am I not consanguineous? Am I not of her blood? Tilly-vally, lady. (II.iii.76-83)

Sir Toby has by consanguinity what Falstaff has to presume on and keep by his wits: "Shall I not take mine ease in mine inn but I shall have my pocket pick'd?" (*I H.IV* III.iii.92-94) So Sir Toby is witty without being as alert as Sir John; he does not need to be:

> *Olivia.* Cousin, cousin, how have you come so early by this lethargy?
>
> *Toby.* Lechery? I defy lechery. There's one at the gate.
>
> *Olivia.* Ay, marry, what is he?
>
> *Toby.* Let him be the devil an he will. I care not! Give me faith, say I. Well, it's all one. (I.v.131-137)

Stage drunkenness, here expressed by wit that lurches catch-as-catch-can, conveys the security of "good life" in such households as Olivia's, the old-fashioned sort that had not given up "housekeeping." Because Toby has "faith"—the faith that goes with belonging—he does not need to worry when Maria teases him about confining himself "within the modest limits of order." "Confine? I'll confine myself no finer than I am" (I.iii.8-11). In his talk as in his clothes, he has the ease of a gentleman whose place in the world is secure, so that, while he can find words like *consanguineous* at will, he can also say "Sneck up!" to Malvolio's accusation that he shows "no respect of persons, places, nor time" (II.iii.99). Sir Toby is the sort of kinsman who would take the lead at such Christmas feasts as Sir Edward Dymoke patronized in Lincolnshire—a Talboys Dymoke.[3] His talk is salted with holiday morals: "I am sure care's an enemy of life" (I.iii.2-3). "Not to be abed before midnight is to be up betimes" (II.iii.1-2). He is like Falstaff in main-

---

[3] The whole encounter between Talboys Dymoke's revellers and the Earl of Lincoln is remarkably like that between Sir Toby's group and Malvolio. . . . The parallels are all the more impressive because no influence or "source" relationship is involved; there must have been many such encounters.

taining saturnalian paradox and in playing impromptu the role of lord
of misrule. But in his whole relation to the world he is fundamentally
different from Prince Hal's great buffoon. Falstaff makes a career of
misrule; Sir Toby uses misrule to show up a careerist.

There is little direct invocation by poetry of the values of heritage
and housekeeping, such as we get of the beneficence of wealth in *The
Merchant of Venice*. But the graciousness of community is conveyed
indirectly by the value put on music and song, as Mr. Van Doren
observes. The Duke's famous opening lines start the play with music.
His hypersensitive estheticism savors strains that have a dying fall and
mixes the senses in appreciation: "like the sweet sound/That breathes
upon a bank of violets" (I.i.5-6). Toby and his friends are more at
ease about "O mistress mine," but equally devoted to music in their
way. (Toby makes fun of such strained appreciation as the Duke's when
he concludes their praises of the clown's voice with "To hear by the
nose, it is dulcet in contagion" II.iii.57-58.) Back at court, in the next
scene, the significance of music in relation to community is suggested
in the Duke's lines about the "old and antique song":

> Mark it, Cesario; it is old and plain.
> The spinsters and the knitters in the sun,
> And the free maids that weave their thread with bones,
> Do use to chant it. It is silly sooth,
> And dallies with the innocence of love
> Like the old age.   (II.iv.44-49)

The wonderful line about the free maids, which throws such firm
stress on "free" by the delayed accent, and then slows up in strong,
regular monosyllables, crystallizes the play's central feeling for freedom
in heritage and community. It is consciously nostalgic; the old age is
seen from the vantage of "these most brisk and giddy-paced times"
(II.iv.6).

Throughout the play a contrast is maintained between the taut, rest-
less, elegant court, where people speak a nervous verse, and the free-
wheeling household of Olivia, where, except for the intense moments
in Olivia's amorous interviews with Cesario, people live in an easy-go-
ing prose. The contrast is another version of pastoral. The household
is more than any one person in it. People keep interrupting each other,
changing their minds, letting their talk run out into foolishness—and
through it all Shakespeare expresses the day-by-day going on of a
shared life:

> *Maria.* Nay, either tell me where thou hast been, or I will not open my lips
> so wide as a bristle may enter in way of thy excuse.   (I.v.1-3)
> *Fabian.* . . . You know he brought me out o' favour with my lady about a
> bear-baiting here.

Toby. To anger him we'll have the bear again . . . (II.v.8-11)
Fabian. Why, we shall make him mad indeed.
Maria. The house will be the quieter. (III.iv.146-147)

Maria's character is a function of the life of "the house"; she moves within it with perfectly selfless tact. "She's a beagle true-bred," says Sir Toby: her part in the housekeeping and its pleasures is a homely but valued kind of "courtiership."

All of the merrymakers show a fine sense of the relations of people, including robust Fabian, and Sir Toby, when he has need. The fool, especially, has this courtly awareness. We see in the first scene that he has to have it to live: he goes far enough in the direction of plain speaking to engage Olivia's unwilling attention, then brings off his thesis that *she* is the fool so neatly that he is forgiven. What Viola praises in the fool's function is just what we should expect in a play about courtesy and liberty:

> This fellow is wise enough to play the fool,
> And to do that well craves a kind of wit.
> He must observe their mood on whom he jests.
> The quality of persons and the time . . . (III.i.67-70)

It is remarkable how little Feste says that is counterstatement in Touch-stone's manner: there is no need for ironic counterstatement, because here the ironies are embodied in the comic butts. Instead what Feste chiefly does is sing and beg—courtly occupations—and radiate in his songs and banter a feeling of liberty based on accepting disillusion. "What's to come is still unsure . . . Youth's a stuff will not endure" (II.iii.50, 53). In *The Merchant of Venice*, it was the gentlefolk who commented "How every fool can play upon the word!" but now it is the fool himself who says, with mock solemnity: "To see this age! A sentence is but a chev'ril glove to a good wit!" (III.i.12-13). He rarely makes the expected move, but conveys by his style how well he knows what moves are expected:

> so that, conclusions to be as kisses, if your four negatives make your two affirmatives, why then, the worse for my friends and the better for my foes.
> *Duke.* Why, this is excellent.
> *Feste.* By my troth, sir, no; though it pleases you to be one of my friends.
> (V.i.24-29)

His feeling for people and their relations comes out most fully when he plays "Sir Topas the curate, who comes to visit Malvolio the luna-tic" (IV.ii.25-26). This is the pastime of "dissembling" in a minister's

STATE COLLEGE
LEARNING CENTER

gown that led to so much trouble for Sir Edward Dymoke's bailiff, John
Craddock the elder.

Viola, who as "nuntio" moves from tense court to relaxed household, has much in common with Feste in the way she talks, or better,
uses talk; but she also commands effortlessly, when there is occasion,
Shakespeare's mature poetic power:

> It gives a very echo to the seat
> Where love is throned.   (II.iv.21-22)

"Thou dost speak masterly," the Duke exclaims—as we must too. Part
of her mastery is that she lets herself go only rarely, choosing occasions that are worthy. Most of the time she keeps her language reined
in, often mocking it as she uses it, in Feste's fashion. Perhaps it is because he finds himself beaten at his own game that he turns on her un-
graciously, as on no one else:

> *Viola.* I warrant thou art a merry fellow and car'st for nothing.
> *Clown.* Not so, sir; I do care for something; but in my conscience, sir, I
> do not care for you. If that be to care for nothing, sir, I would it would
> make you invisible.   (III.i.32-35)

Once when she is mocking the elaborate language of compliment,
greeting Olivia with "the heavens rain odors on you," Sir Andrew over-
hears and is much impressed: "That youth's a rare courtier. 'Rain
odors'—well" (III.i.97-98). He plans to get her fancy words by heart.
Of course, as a rare courtier, she precisely does *not* commit herself to
such high-flown, Osric-style expressions. Her constant shifting of tone
in response to the situation goes with her manipulation of her role in
disguise, so that instead of simply listening to her speak, we watch her
conduct her speech, and through it feel her secure sense of proportion
and her easy, alert consciousness: "To one of your receiving," says
Olivia, "enough is shown" (III.i.131-132).

Olivia says that "it was never merry world/Since lowly feigning was
called compliment" (III.i.109-110). As Sir Toby is the spokesman and
guardian of that merry world, Malvolio is its antagonist. He shows his
relation to festivity at once by the way he responds to Feste, and Olivia
points the moral: he is "sick of self-love" and tastes "with a distempered appetite." He is not "generous, guiltless, and of free disposition."
Of course, nothing is more helpful, to get revelry to boil up, than
somebody trying to keep the lid on—whatever his personal qualities.
But the "stubborn and uncourteous parts" in Malvolio's character, to
which Fabian refers in justifying the "device," are precisely those qualities which liberty shows up. Malvolio wants "to confine himself finer
than he is," to paraphrase Toby in reverse: he practices behavior to

his own shadow. His language is full of pompous polysyllables, of elaborate syntax deploying synonyms:

> Do ye make an alehouse of my lady's house, that ye squeak out your coziers' catches without any mitigation or remorse of voice? Is there no respect of place, persons, nor time in you? (II.iii.96-99)

In "loving" his mistress, as Cesario her master, he is a kind of foil, bringing out her genuine, free impulse by the contrast he furnishes. He does not desire Olivia's person; *that* desire, even in a steward, would be sympathetically regarded, though not of course encouraged, by a Twelfth Night mood. What he wants is "to be count Malvolio," with "a demure travel of regard—telling them I know my place, as I would they should theirs" (II.v.59-61). His secret wish is to violate decorum himself, then relish to the full its power over others. No wonder he has not a free disposition when he has such imaginations to keep under! When the sport betrays him into a revelation of them, part of the vengeance taken is to make him try to be festive, in yellow stockings, and crossgartered, and smiling "his face into more lines than is in the new map with the augmentation of the Indies" (III.ii.91-93). Maria's letter *tells* him to go brave, be gallant, take liberties! And when we see him "acting this in an obedient hope" (as he puts it later), he is anything but free: "This does make some obstruction of the blood, this cross-gartering . . ." (III.iv.21-23).

In his "impossible passages of grossness," he is the profane intruder trying to steal part of the initiates' feast by disguising himself as one of them—only to be caught and tormented for his profanation. As with Shylock, there is potential pathos in his bafflement, especially when Shakespeare uses to the limit the conjuring of devils out of a sane man, a device which he had employed hilariously in *The Comedy of Errors*. There is no way to settle just how much of Malvolio's pathos should be allowed to come through when he is down and out in the dark hole. Most people now agree that Charles Lamb's sympathy for the steward's enterprise and commiseration for his sorrows is a romantic and bourgeois distortion. But he is certainly pathetic, if one thinks about it, because he is so utterly cut off from everyone else by his anxious self-love. He lacks the freedom which makes Viola so perceptive, and is correspondingly oblivious:

> *Olivia.* What kind o' man is he?
> *Malvolio.* Why, of mankind. (I.v.159-160)

He is too busy carrying out his mistress' instructions about privacy to notice that she is bored with it, as later he is too busy doing her errand with the ring to notice that it is a love token. He is imprisoned in his own virtues, so that there is sense as well as nonsense in the fool's

"I say there is no darkness but ignorance, in which thou art more puzzled than the Egyptians in their fog" (IV.ii.46-49). The dark house is,
without any straining, a symbol: when Malvolio protests about Pythagoras, "I think nobly of the soul and no way approve his opinion,"
the clown's response in "Remain thou in darkness." The pack of them
are wanton and unreasonable in tormenting him; but his reasonable-
ness will never let him out into "the air; . . . the glorious sun"
(IV.ii.1) which they enjoy together. To play the dark-house scene for
pathos, instead of making fun out of the pathos, or at any rate out of
most of the pathos, is to ignore the dry comic light which shows up
Malvolio's virtuousness as a self-limiting automatism.

Malvolio has been called a satirical portrait of the Puritan spirit,
and there is some truth in the notion. But he is not hostile to holiday
because he is a Puritan; he is like a Puritan because he is hostile to
holiday. Shakespeare even mocks, in passing, the thoughtless, fashionable antipathy to Puritans current among gallants. Sir Andrew responds to Maria's "sometimes he is a kind of Puritan," with "if I
thought that, I'd beat him like a dog" (II.iii.151-153). "The devil a
Puritan he is, or anything constantly," Maria observes candidly, "but a
time-pleaser" (II.iii.159-160). Shakespeare's two greatest comic butts,
Malvolio and Shylock, express basic human attitudes which were at
work in the commercial revolution, the new values whose development
R. H. Tawney described in *Religion and the Rise of Capitalism*. But
both figures are conceived at a level of esthetic abstraction which makes
it inappropriate to identify them with specific social groups in the
mingled actualities of history: Shylock, embodying ruthless money
power, is no more to be equated with actual bankers than Malvolio,
who has something of the Puritan ethic, is to be thought of as a portrait of actual Puritans. Yet, seen in the perspective of literary and social history, there is a curious appropriateness in Malvolio's presence,
as a kind of foreign body to be expelled by laughter, in Shakespeare's
last free-and-easy festive comedy. He is a man of business, and, it is
passingly suggested, a hard one; he is or would like to be a rising man,
and to rise he *uses* sobriety and morality. One could moralize the spec-
tacle by observing that, in the long run, in the 1640's, Malvolio *was*
revenged on the whole pack of them.

But Shakespeare's comedy remains, long after 1640, to move audiences through release to clarification, making distinctions between
false care and true freedom and realizing anew, for successive generations, powers in human nature and society which make good the risks
of courtesy and liberty. And this without blinking the fact that "the
rain it raineth every day."

Charles Lamb and the Tragic Malvolio

by Sylvan Barnet

In February, April, and October, 1822, *The London Magazine* published three articles by Charles Lamb on the actors of previous decades. These essays, later revised and published in *Elia,* are among the most sensitive nineteenth century studies of the art of acting. Critical attention, beginning with Macaulay's comments on Lamb included in a review of Leigh Hunt's edition of several Restoration dramatists, has concentrated, for the most part, upon the essay which was called, in its revised version, "On the Artificial Comedy of the Last Century." The two other essays have received almost no attention, though they are not merely interesting in themselves, but are of first importance in understanding Lamb's theory of acting, which is inextricably related to his theory of the nature of drama. The first of them, "On Some of the Old Actors," [1] is largely devoted to a recollection of the Malvolio of Robert Bensley, a role which Lamb regarded as having tragic affinities. "I confess," he wrote, "that I never saw the catastrophe of this character, while Bensley played it, without a kind of tragic interest." This study will examine Lamb's interpretation of the play, and his comments on Bensley's performance.

Although Bensley enjoyed a good reputation during his years on the stage, he seems not to have been regarded as a leading actor by any critic but Lamb. He played numerous roles both in comedy and in tragedy, was often favorably mentioned, but never achieved the stature of a star actor, in an age when the theatrical firmament was adorned with Mrs. Siddons and John Kemble, and a host of lesser lights. Unlike so many of his colleagues, he was not the subject of the customary two-volume biography, nor has modern theatrical research expended much effort on him. E. V. Lucas, in his notes to Lamb's essay, merely observes that "G. H. Boaden [*sic*] and George Colman both bear out Lamb's eulogy of Bensley as Malvolio but otherwise he is not the sub-

---

[1] *Works of Charles and Mary Lamb,* ed. E. V. Lucas (London, 1903-1905), II, 132-141. All subsequent quotations not otherwise cited are from this essay.

ject of much praise." [2] Yet his Malvolio, or rather Lamb's account of his tragic Malvolio, has had a great effect upon the stage history of the play. No less an actor than Sir Henry Irving (who had never seen the play performed) seems to have derived a good part of his interpretation of the role from Lamb's essay, and, no doubt, fragments of Bensley have survived the years in the performances of a number of lesser Malvolios. If he has thus survived, however, he has not always been treated with the honor which Lamb bestowed upon him. He has represented, for most twentieth century scholars and critics, Romantic sentimentalism at its worst. Under the influence of "the Romantic point of view," writes John Draper, Malvolio's "character became stuff of serious drama rather than of satiric comedy of manners. Charles Lamb and the actor Bensley seem to have set this style. Of course, it throws the part quite out of focus, spoils our enjoyment of Maria's stratagem, precludes poetic justice in the play; and, while it leaves in comic vein the plots of Olivia's marriage and Maria's, it makes the gulling of Malvolio an unresolved tragedy." [3] Now, Draper implies that there is a single Romantic interpretation of the role. I suggest that the evidence leads us to a contrary conclusion. Closest to Lamb in his view of *Twelfth Night* is Hazlitt, who was a bit upset at the fun made of Malvolio. "If poor Malvolio's treatment afterwards is a little hard, poetical justice is done in the uneasiness which Olivia suffers on account of her mistaken attachment to Cesario." [4] Aware that in comedy poetic justice must reign, Hazlitt has sought by his interpretation of Olivia to redress the balance which he overset when he took Malvolio too seriously. But besides Lamb, no Romantic went, in his sympathy for Malvolio, even as far as Hazlitt. And Hazlitt himself concentrated attention not on the Steward, but upon the romantic aspects of the play, which was, he wrote, "full of sweetness and pleasantry. It is perhaps too good-natured for comedy. It has little satire, and no spleen. . . . It makes us laugh at the follies of mankind, not despise them, and still less bear any ill will towards them." [5] Leigh Hunt seems never to have thought of a tragic Malvolio,[6] De Quincey ignored the play, and Coleridge confined himself to observations on the title and a few lines of the comedy. The Romantic *Twelfth Night,* in short, is merely Lamb's *Twelfth Night* and—perhaps—Bensley's.

Shakespeare's play is, of course, a romantic comedy, with even less of a threat to a happy outcome than there is in his other plays in this

[2] *Ibid.,* II, 393.
[3] *The "Twelfth Night" of Shakespeare's Audience* (Stanford, 1950), p. 87.
[4] *The Complete Works,* ed. P. P. Howe (London, 1930-1934), IV, 318.
[5] *Ibid.,* IV, 313. The word "romantic," as opposed to "Romantic," has the ordinary meaning, "fanciful."
[6] See *Leigh Hunt's Dramatic Criticism,* ed. Laurence Houston Houtchens and Carolyn Washburn Houtchens (New York, 1949), pp. 41-44, 227-231.

genre. No Shylock whets his knife, no Don John lurks malignantly in the shadows; indeed, there is not even a Charles who threatens to crack an Orlando's ribs. When Davenant revived *Twelfth Night* in 1661, he probably minimized the love story and played up the farcical elements. Betterton was his Sir Toby, while Malvolio was assigned to Thomas Lovel, an unimportant actor.[7] The nineteenth century emphasis on Malvolio is now sometimes contrasted unfavorably with the conjectured Restoration version, but there is really no valid reason for assuming that the interpretations of the age of Charles II provide a fair touchstone. Late seventeenth century stage traditions, in fact, are particularly useless in helping to interpret Shakespeare's romantic comedies, for the Restoration took little pleasure in these dramas. Earlier spectators, however, did find that Malvolio was a major figure (though not a tragic one) in the play. When John Manningham of the Middle Temple confided to his diary his comments on the play, which he saw following the feast of February 2, 1602, he did not remark on the love of Viola for Orsino, but on the good trick of making a steward think his mistress was in love with him, and then making the poor gull believe that others in the household thought him mad. And several decades later Charles I crossed out the title of the play in the royal copy of the Second Folio (1632), and replaced it with "Malvolio." In short, the earliest evidence we have, scanty though it is, indicates that the Steward was the center of interest, while later evidence (even more scanty) suggests that during the Restoration he was not. Certainly he was never conceived tragically before the late eighteenth century, and I shall endeavor to show that in the early nineteenth century Lamb was unique in his conception of the part, and thus is largely responsible for the tragic Malvolio.

The play is not a tragedy, and the love-plot is, as I have indicated, even less threatened than in some of Shakespeare's other romantic comedies, for it has no villain. H. V. Dyson, however, in an interesting essay, finds the stuff of tragedy existing potentially in the isolation which Antonio endures when he is abandoned by the youth whom he has befriended.[8] And Logan Pearsall Smith, always a sensitive student of Shakespeare, found that

> the increase of Shakespeare's creative power shows itself, not only in the greater number of living people he puts upon the stage, . . . but also in the greater depth and complexity of their characters. . . . Certain figures, like Shylock and Malvolio, assume almost tragic proportions, and foreshadowing the tormented souls of the later tragedies, put the gay music of the comedies a little out of tune.[9]

[7] See Hazelton Spencer, *Shakespeare Improved* (Cambridge, Mass., 1927), pp. 70-71.
[8] "The Emergence of Shakespeare's Tragedy," *Proceedings of the British Academy*, XXXVI (1950), 90-91.
[9] *On Reading Shakespeare* (London, 1933), pp. 95-96. See also p. 112.

But if the music is out of tune, if the plot is not ultimately harmonious, the piece is not an esthetic success. Smith's reading of the play, then, lessens its value, although his aim is to demonstrate that the comedy is greater than its predecessors. An interpretation which tells us that a man who has written several great comedies now no longer perceives the decorum necessary to the genre, is, I think, not necessarily false, but open to grave suspicion.

The divisions between comedy and tragedy, however helpful, can be misleading. In the *Philebus* Plato held that the poet depicts both comedy and tragedy, and that the spectator feels both pleasure and pain. And both genres deal, but in somewhat different ways, with the problem of man's adaptation to his environment. Malvolio is potentially tragic, for he finds that past modes of behavior are no longer suitable, no longer meaningful in his present relationship with the world. His self-love is no longer adequate. In tragedy, the protagonist comes to some such realization, and by a heroic, and exhausting, endeavor, readjusts the balance. But in *Twelfth Night* Malvolio rejects the challenge to alter himself, and grotesquely continues to defy his antagonists, who are not villains of great power, but jovial tipplers. The struggle is unworthy as well as unheroic. Our sympathies are all with Malvolio's foes, who represent a way of life which gains, at least within the playhouse, our approval. The world of Goneril and Regan, of King Claudius, of Iago, we reject, and our sympathy goes out to the man partly entrapped in it. But Illyria is another thing, and he who would war against it forfeits our approval, since he has forfeited his love of humanity.

Before we consider the esthetics of the play in any greater detail, it is necessary that we have as clear an idea as possible of Bensley's interpretation of Malvolio. Bensley's art survives chiefly in Lamb's essay, and if Garrick was somewhat too pessimistic when he wrote

> Nor Pen nor Pencil can the Actor save,
> The Art and Artist, share one common Grave,

we must nevertheless grant that Bensley has acquired only a dubious immortality, and, in fact, he would have endured less abuse from anti-Romantic critics had he escaped Lamb's pen. In any event, Lamb has given us the fullest and best-written account of Bensley, and any discussion of him must begin with Lamb's essay. Now, even when we grant that an actor cannot give the identical performance twice, and that Bensley may have consciously, as well as unconsciously, altered his style over the years, in the absence of further evidence we must assume that Lamb's picture was not a candid snapshot of an unusual incident, but rather a careful painting, done from life, of a frequently observed subject. Lamb's whole essay implies that he often, or at least several times, saw Malvolio played by Bensley, who always acted the part in a certain manner. After discussing Bensley's Iago and Hotspur, he writes:

> The part of Malvolio, in the Twelfth Night, was performed by Bensley, with a richness and a dignity, of which (to judge from some recent castings of that character) the very tradition must be worn out from the stage. . . . Malvolio is not essentially ludicrous. He becomes comic but by accident. He is cold, austere, repelling; but dignified, consistent, and, for what appears, rather of an overstretched morality. Maria describes him as a sort of Puritan; and he might have worn his gold chain with honor in one of our old round-head families, in the service of a Lambert, or a Lady Fairfax. But his morality and his manners are misplaced in Illyria. He is opposed to the proper *levities* of the piece, and falls in the unequal contest. Still his pride, or his gravity (call it which you will), is inherent, and native to the man, not mock or affected, which latter only are the fit objects to excite laughter. His quality is at the best unlovely, but neither buffoon nor contemptible. . . . Olivia, at the first indication of his supposed madness, declares that she "would not have him miscarry for half her dowry." Does this look as if the character was meant to appear little or insignificant? Once, indeed, she accuses him to his face—of what?—of being "sick of self-love,"—but with a gentleness and considerateness which could not have been, if she had not thought that this particular infirmity shaded some virtues. His rebuke to the knight, and his sottish revelers, is sensible and spirited.

To this already intolerable deal of quotation, I must add another paragraph. Having set forth his own interpretation of the role, Lamb shifts to a discussion of Bensley:

> Bensley, accordingly, threw over the part an air of Spanish loftiness. He looked, spake, and moved like an old Castilian. He was starch, spruce, opinionated, but his superstructure of pride seemed bottomed upon a sense of worth. There was something in it beyond the coxcomb. . . . O! shake not the castles of his pride—endure yet for a season bright moments of confidence—"stand still ye watches of the element," that Malvolio may be still in fancy fair Olivia's lord—but fate and retribution say no—I hear the mischievous titter of Maria—the witty taunts of Sir Toby—the still more insupportable triumph of the foolish knight —the counterfeit Sir Topas is unmasked—and "thus the whirligig of time," as the true clown hath it, "brings in his revenges." I confess that I never saw the catastrophe of this character, while Bensley played it, without a kind of tragic interest.

Lamb, in brief, found great dignity and merit in Malvolio, and though he granted that the Steward was flawed with pride, he held that "if an unseasonable reflection of morality obtruded itself, it was a

deep sense of the pitiable infirmity of man's nature, that can lay him
open to such frenzies—but in truth you rather admired than pitied
the lunacy while it lasted—you felt that an hour of such mistake was
worth an age with the eyes open."

The pattern which Lamb establishes is clearly a tragic one. A man
of considerable worth falls from weal to woe, through an infirmity in
his nature, and even in his infirmity there is a kind of greatness. Fur-
thermore, his fall inspires us to think of the weakness and yet the
majesty of human nature. Lamb asserts that Bensley's playing, more
than earlier or later performances, paralleled this interpretation. Since
Bensley's death, writes Lamb, the tradition seems to have vanished.
And there is no evidence that before Bensley played the role any actor
or critic looked at the part in just this way. Now, although Lamb's
playgoing began before he was six, with a visit to Drury Lane in 1780,
he did not attend the theater with any regularity until seven or eight
years later. As Lamb was only twenty-one when Bensley retired from
the stage on May 6, 1796, he was by no means a mature critic during
Bensley's acting career. His account of *Twelfth Night*, written more
than a quarter of a century after Bensley had retired, is the work of
a sophisticated critic (however wrongheaded we feel the essay may be),
and is based more on nostalgic reminiscence than on fresh observation.
Theater critics generally develop excellent memories for stage business,
and their reports of scenery, action, gesture in plays they witnessed in
times long past are frequently amazingly accurate. But despite the accuracy of the details their own interpretation inevitably colors the
whole performance. Before we examine the scanty contemporary evidence which supplements Lamb's essay, we should first note that Lamb
admits that the Malvolios of his own day (that is, the early nineteenth
century) are not in the Bensley tradition. And Samuel Phelps, perhaps
the greatest actor between Macready and Irving, owed little to his interpretation of Malvolio to Lamb's picture of Bensley's conception.
Henry Morley, for example, laid emphasis upon the fact that Phelps's
Malvolio, despite his Spanish dignity (here the critic is probably echo-
ing Lamb), is a pompous fool whose fall excites only laughter,[10] and
Bayle Bernard wrote that "we have nothing pleasanter or heartier
in the whole round of comic fiction than the conspiracy against Malvolio, or the enforced combat of the two cowards, poor Sir Andrew and
the Page." [11] These observations may be only straws in the wind, but
they show us with fair accuracy the kind of Malvolio which the middle
nineteenth century expected and received. Henry Irving's Malvolio

---

[10] See W. May Phelps, *The Life and Life-Work of Samuel Phelps* (London, 1886),
p. 159. Morley's reference to "a Spanish king" and "the Spanish-looking steward"
must not be taken out of context. He clearly regarded Malvolio (in Phelps's performance) as a comic figure who is both a timeserver and a self-deceiving gull.
[11] *Ibid.*, p. 160.

(1884) seems to have been the first interpretation obviously based on Lamb's essay, and later E. H. Sothern's performance was even more tragic, but these productions take us beyond the chronological limits of historical Romanticism, into the nebulous realm of the influence of Romanticism on Victorian culture.

Most of Bensley's contemporaries who wrote about him at all praised his Malvolio. For example, the author of *Memoirs of Mrs. Crouch* observed that "Mr. Bensley, in the vain fantastical Malvolio, was excellent," [12] and John Adolphus, in his biography of John Bannister, alluded to "Bensley's solemn deportment and ludicrous gullibility in Malvolio." [13] If we are accustomed to seeing Bensley only through Lamb's eyes, these words have a strange sound. The "vain, fantastical Malvolio" of the *Memoirs of Mrs. Crouch* no more accords with Lamb's Steward of "richness and dignity" than does the ludicrous and gullible fellow in the *Memoirs of John Bannister*. Now, these actors knew Bensley intimately, and the testimony in their biographies merits serious attention. Lamb wrote about Bensley more fully, and with more artistry, but not necessarily more accurately. Mrs. Crouch played Olivia to Bensley's Malvolio at Drury Lane, and thus knew his performance at first hand, and Bannister's testimony is especially significant, for he had observed Bensley so closely that for a while he mimicked him when he played Dick, the stagestruck youth, in Arthur Murphy's *The Apprentice*. Dick's rendition of dramatic bits, when played by Bannister, was in the odd manner of Bensley, for Bannister (and presumably the theater-going public) found that in Bensley "there was a peculiar glare in his eye, an occasional prominency in his gait, and a peculiar tone in his voice, easily to be imitated in a most striking manner." [14] Bensley's natural defects are often mentioned. John Taylor observed that "his voice was rough, and had no variety," [15] and its tones "were grave and often nasal." [16] Bensley's stiffness was also mentioned frequently, but most commentators add that although he triumphed over these handicaps, they were not always liabilities. Genest wrote that "his voice and manner were well suited to Malvolio," [17] and Taylor said that all his peculiarities "operated in his favour in the part of Malvolio." [18] Similarly, George Colman the Younger held that Bensley's stalk, stiffness, and nasal twang aided him in "his personification of Malvolio, the starch and conceited Steward." [19]

[12] M. J. Young, *Memoirs of Mrs. Crouch* (London, 1806), II, 35.
[13] *Memoirs of John Bannister* (London, 1839), I, 129.
[14] *Ibid.*, I, 30.
[15] *Records of My Life* (London, 1932) , I, 431.
[16] *Ibid.*, II, 143.
[17] *Some Account of the English Stage* (Bath, 1832), VII, 252.
[18] *Records of My Life*, II, 143.
[19] *Random Records* (London, 1830), II, 7.

The dignity which Lamb felt invested Bensley, Bensley's contemporaries often felt was comic. The testimonies from which I have quoted
indicate over and over that his Malvolio was a grotesque figure, not
a serious or tragic one. His gravity was a symbol of his conceit, of his
self-love, and indeed, Bensley seems to have possessed, even off the
stage, a gravity which aroused amusement. I have already alluded to
Bannister's imitation of him, but even more significant is the testimony
of a close friend, Michael Kelly. Bensley, Kelly wrote, "had a manner
of rolling his eyes when speaking; and a habit, whenever he entered
the green-room, of stirring the fire with great ceremony, secundem ar-
tem, in which habit, I was in the habit of imitating him; he caught me
once in the very fact, and joined heartily in the laugh against himself." [20] Bensley was often praised for his intelligence and gentlemanliness, but his virtues and vices seem to have been so intermingled that
this gentlemanliness was often the subject of good-natured fun, and
the man's defects were the actor's excellences. One more account of
his Malvolio must be given, and in some ways it is the most significant.
James Boaden, the prolific theatrical biographer, was not a brilliant or
penetrating critic, but he was, on the whole, an accurate recorder of
the stage. His most lengthy comment on Bensley is, like other descrip-
tions of the actor, full of praise for his Malvolio, and yet at variance
with Lamb's essay:

> Bensley and Aiken were both manly; but for pleasantry, alas! it became
> *satire* in passing their lips. I never laughed with Bensley but once, and
> then he represented Malvolio, in which, I thought him perfection.
> Bensley had been a soldier, yet his stage walk eternally reminded you of
> the *"one, two, three, hop,"* of the dancing-master; this scientific progress
> of legs, in yellow stockings, most villainously cross-gartered, with a hor-
> rible laugh of ugly conceit to top the whole, rendered him Shakespeare's
> Malvolio at all points.[21]

It is interesting to note that Boaden not only regarded Bensley's Malvolio as amusing, but believed that the actor had perfectly captured
the comic nature of the part.

Lamb's interpretation of Bensley as Malvolio not only fails to cor-
respond with contemporary opinions, but is strangely inconsistent with
his own theory of comedy. As he realized (even in "On the Artificial
Comedy of the Last Century"), comedy is frequently a light-hearted
protest against some of its characters. Prudish parents, jealous hus-
bands, misers, and all such troublemakers, are held up to derision, and
the ideal comic world agrees with Sir Toby Belch that "care's an enemy to life." Those who intrude, however, into the world of comedy

[20] *Reminiscences* (London, 1826), II, 89.
[21] *The Life of Mrs. Jordan* (London, 1831), I, 124.

must not be taken too seriously, and must ultimately be dismissed with a laugh and a shrug. The subjects of mirth in art are, in real life, not necessarily amusing, but they are deviations from the norm. Lamb knew that some of these deviations, the miser, for example, depicted realistically on the stage would not afford laughter, and he wisely suggested that the actor must not be too natural, but, indeed, must make his role engaging by presenting a cartoon of his subject. The real miser, the real jealous husband, however, though not always amusing, is, by his deviation, out of place even in the real world, for his excessive attention to a particular matter sets him apart from other men. He does not quite "fit" in real life, and comedy capitalizes on his incompatibility. But Lamb suggests that Malvolios are necessary and at home in the real world, and that Shakespeare's Steward is comic only because he has been taken out of the realm of reality and thrust into the fairyland of Illyria. Such an interpretation eliminates or at best minimizes both Malvolio's self-love and his consequent attempt to foist his own ideas upon others. It sees in him only a diligent man thrust into a world free from worry, and it overlooks the fact that his diligence is chiefly exerted in self-advancement. In short, I suggest that Malvolio is intrinsically comic, a deviation from the norm of life, and in Illyria, of course he is doubly so. Malvolio seeking to rise in the social scale, Malvolio fondling his chain and imagining it to be some rich jewel— these are comic, and not only in Illyria. Lamb merely grants that Malvolio is out of place in Illyria, and hence he gives him a great measure of sympathy. In fact, so great is his sympathy that he shifts the object of value from Illyria to Malvolio, and thus brings us into the tragic realm, where the hero often is superior to his environment.

Lamb's discussion of Bensley, I think, is Lamb writing of his own Malvolio, rather than of Bensley's. The evidence of Bensley's contemporaries clearly suggests that the actor's Malvolio was not that which Lamb depicted twenty-six years after Bensley had retired. Perhaps Lamb's memory was partly at fault, but the distortion also arises, I think, from his creative faculty. His interpretation of the play is wrong, but it is an interpretation which could only be produced by a sensitive mind in contact with a great work of art. Drama critics have not infrequently attributed, unconsciously, their interpretations of a role to the actor who performed the part. C. E. Montague's brilliant essay on *Richard II*, which has received general acceptance by Shakespearean critics, credited Frank Benson with an interpretation which Benson himself disavowed.[22] Similarly, Lamb, I think, transferred his own view of Malvolio to the actor who had delighted him in his youth.[23]

[22] See James Agate, *The Later Ego* (New York, 1951), pp. 584-585.
[23] In a letter to John Rickman (*Letters of Charles Lamb, to Which are Added Those of His Sister Mary Lamb*, ed. E. V. Lucas [London, 1935], I, 273), Lamb makes

In conclusion, one final, and extremely tentative, observation might be made. I have endeavored to show that Lamb's view of Malvolio is not an accurate picture of Bensley, nor is it typical of Romantic criticism of the play. Is it possible that his inability to laugh at Malvolio, his failure to appreciate the comic aspects of the figure, was—at least in part—due to the fact that his own father was a household servant? We know very little about John Lamb, but there is no doubt that he was not only Samuel Salt's clerk, but his valet, and was entrusted with the management of his employer's house. I am not suggesting that he resembled Malvolio in character, but only in profession. Like Malvolio, he had considerable responsibilities, for Salt, according to Lamb's picture of him in "The Old Benchers of the Inner Temple," seems to have been a good-natured man, but careful neither of his appearance nor of his lodgings. Charles Lamb, we should recall, emphasized the point that our judgment of Malvolio must take into consideration the responsibilities which Olivia by her sentimentality, and Sir Toby by his roistering, allowed to fall on the Steward's shoulders.[24] I do not wish to press the suggestion further, but I feel that Lamb's serious treatment of Malvolio may perhaps have been influenced by his own family background. The son of a responsible servant might possibly fail to see the humor in the discomforting of a major-domo. In any event, I suggest that Lamb's brilliant but wrong interpretation of *Twelfth Night* is not Bensley's, not the age's, but Lamb's own.

---

an interesting allusion to Malvolio. He writes of William Godwin, who was then courting Mary Jane Clairmont: "He bows when he is spoke to, and smiles without occasion, and wriggles as fantastically as Malvolio." Written in 1801, this is a brief but distinctly unfavorable interpretation of the role, and one which Lamb had rejected by the time he wrote his essay.

[24] G. A. Bonnard, in "Le Portrait de Samuel Salt," *Études anglaises*, V (1952), 202-204, emphasizes Lamb's conjecture that Salt's introspection and neglect of his dwelling are explicable if we recall that he was a widower. Olivia, too, is in mourning (though for a brother, not a husband), and thus the parallel between Malvolio's employer and John Lamb's is intensified.

Shakespeare's Confluence of Tragedy and Comedy: *Twelfth Night* and *King Lear*

by Julian Markels

. . . The word "fool" runs through a spectrum of meanings throughout the play [*King Lear*], as when in successive speeches Lear calls the
world a "great stage of fools" and himself "The natural fool of fortune." The Fool himself encompasses this range of meaning in a song
that provides a microscopic statement of almost the whole idea of *King
Lear*:

> That sir which serves and seeks for gain,
>   And follows but for form,
> Will pack when it begins to rain,
>   And leave thee in the storm.
> But I will tarry; the fool will stay,
>   And let the wise man fly.
> The knave turns fool that runs away;
>   The fool no knave, perdy.

Like the protean word "nature," "fool" is a major vehicle of thought
in this most philosophic of Shakespeare's plays; and it is conceptually
related to "nature" by inseparable bonds of meaning even at the
farthest reaches of the play's doctrine. That is surely a large part for a
comic concept in so terrifying a tragedy as *King Lear*.

The relation between Lear and his Fool which generates this meaning has been precisely anticipated in the opening dialogue between
Olivia and her Fool in *Twelfth Night* (I.v). Lear's Fool bounces on to
the stage offering his coxcomb to Kent for taking Lear's part, and then
throughout two acts proposes a series of conundrums uniformly designed to show Lear a fool for giving his kingdom to his daughters.
Olivia's Fool, who has absented himself from her household ever since

"Shakespeare's Confluence of Tragedy and Comedy: Twelfth Night *and* King
Lear" *by Julian Markels. Slightly abridged for this edition. From the* Shakespeare
Quarterly, *XV (1964), 75-88. Copyright © 1964 by the Shakespeare Association of
America. Reprinted by permission of Julian Markels and the Shakespeare Association
of America.*

she took a vow to mourn her brother's death for seven years, gets back
in her good graces by proving her a fool:

> *Clown.* Good madonna, why mourn'st thou?
> *Olivia.* Good clown, for my brother's death.
> *Clown.* I think his soul is in hell, madonna.
> *Olivia.* I know his soul is in heaven, fool.
> *Clown.* The more fool, madonna, to mourn for your brother's soul, being
> in heaven. Take away the fool, gentlemen.
> *Olivia.* What think you of this fool, Malvolio? Doth he not mend?

Malvolio, of course, thinks not, and soon explains why:

> *Malvolio.* I marvel that your ladyship takes delight in such a barren rascal.
> I saw him put down the other day with an ordinary fool that has no
> more brain than a stone. Look you now, he's out of his guard already.
> Unless you laugh and minister occasion to him, he is gagged. *I protest I*
> *take these wise men that crow so at these set kind of fools no better than*
> *the fools' zanies.*
> *Olivia.* O, you are sick of self-love, Malvolio, and taste with a distempered
> appetite. To be generous, guiltless, and of free disposition, is to take
> those things for birdbolts that you deem cannon bullets. *There is no*
> *slander in an allowed fool, though he do nothing but rail; nor no rail-*
> *ing in a known discreet man, though he do nothing but reprove.*[1]

This passage is packed with relevant matter. We may begin by re-
minding ourselves how it expresses the social function of the domestic
fool, whom Olivia here calls "allowed" and Goneril in *King Lear* calls
"all-licensed." He is a household servant whose address to his master
is permitted a degree of freedom that would be considered slanderous
in anybody else, because his purpose is to mend his master's follies.
When Olivia asks whether the Fool does not "mend," probably she
means improve in the performance of his vocation, although it has
been suggested that she means "make amends" for his long absence
from her household. But in either case the word in context means
more than Olivia intends: in catechizing his mistress, the Fool attempts
to mend her distempered appetite for mourning. He is trying to recall
her from a violation of propriety, custom, and good sense, just as Lear's
Fool does, and as Olivia herself is to do with Malvolio and Sir Toby.

   In performing this corrective social function, the domestic fool wins
the wise man's praise, a fact which Malvolio cannot understand. Olivia,
having just been mended into "fool" herself, now undertakes the Fool's
function with Malvolio. She affirms by implication that social custom
and the cosmic scheme of life are consistent with one another, and that

---

[1] All italics within Shakespearian quotations are mine.

this harmony should be perfectly evident to anyone not sick of self-love and thereby out of tune both with custom and with life. If there is no slander in an allowed fool, that is because of the artifice of social institutions whose creature he is: the Fool's words are licensed by the fiat of the social order. But there is no railing in a "known discreet man" only because his discretion has its source outside social institutions in what we can properly call Nature herself. If his reproofs cannot be mistaken for railing, that is not simply because society has so contrived the rules of the game. Society has not invented his wisdom, it has discovered it: the wise man's words are licensed because they are *known* to be discreet, because society looks beyond itself to discover a pattern of wisdom and hence of words by which to order itself. Thus the wise man's discretion guarantees society, whose custom licenses the Fool's words, which in turn aspire to keep custom aligned with discretion and the social fabric mended. "Marry, here's grace and codpiece; that's a wise man and a fool. . . ."

From beginning to end, the idea of clothing is central to both Lear's and Malvolio's interpretation of their spiritual experience. In the full frenzy of his madness, Lear makes one speech—the one which Edgar calls "Reason in madness"—in which he describes how clothes may be used not to accommodate the bare forked animal which is natural man, but to cover by their gorgeousness discommoding violations of human justice and social order. This speech is equally a reflection upon Lear's "overdressing" at the beginning of the play, and upon Malvolio's fantasy of grandeur just before he picks up the fatal letter. I place Lear's and Malvolio's speeches together in order to illustrate the relationship:

Lear. . . . .
> Through tattered clothes small vices do appear;
> Robes and furred gowns hide all. Plate sin with gold,
> And the strong lance of justice hurtless breaks;
> Arm it in rags, a pygmy's straw does pierce it.
> None does offend, none—I say none! I'll able 'em.

Malvolio. To be Count Malvolio. There is example for't. *The Lady of the Strachy married the yeoman of the wardrobe.* Having been three months married to her, sitting in my state—Calling my officers about me, *in my branched velvet gown;* having come from a day-bed, where I have left Olivia sleeping—*And then to have the humour of state;* and after a demure travel of regard, telling them I know my place, as I would they should do theirs, to ask for my kinsman Toby—Seven of my people, with an obedient start, make out for him. I frown the while, and perchance wind up my watch, or play with my—some rich jewel. Toby approaches: curtsies there to me—I extend my hand to him thus, quenching my familiar smile with an austere regard of control—Saying, 'Cousin Toby, *my fortunes having cast me on your niece, give me this prerogative of speech.* You must amend your drunkeness [*sic*].' [2]

The "humour of state," as Malvolio imagines it, is capricious and arbitrary both in its acquisition and its exercise. It is conferred automatically upon him who wears the "branched velvet gown," and becomes a form of playacting designed to puff the ego. It alights upon Toby's drunkenness in order to satisfy Malvolio's vanity rather than any principle of decorum or justice. In a word, for similarly egotistical motives, Malvolio dreams himself into the exact situation and conduct of Lear in the opening scene. Lear exercises a capricious "humour of state" in demanding from his daughters protestations of love merely to please his personal vanity. We sympathize, of course, with his original wish to divide his kingdom and live out his remaining life unburdened by public cares; and Shakespeare has taken great pains to make us sympathize with Malvolio's underlying desire to correct Toby's conduct. But we have been persuaded to approve their ends only so that we may perceive more clearly the error of their means. Both men proceed on the assumption that "Robes and furred gowns hide all." This assumption rips the social fabric, and forces both men eventually to reap the whirlwind.

Beyond Lear himself, there is still another way in which a concern with clothes links the two plays. When Lear encounters the half-naked Edgar on the heath and asks him what he has been, Edgar replies:

A servingman, proud in heart and mind; that curled my hair, wore gloves in my cap; served the lust of my mistress' heart, and did the act of darkness with her. . . .

To explain the cause of his undoing, Edgar attributes to his former self aspirations for which Malvolio becomes a comic butt. This former self is of course fictitious; but in *King Lear* Shakespeare provides us with its living image in Goneril's servant Oswald, a counterpart to Malvolio of whom Kent says, "A tailor made thee." Oswald too is an *arriviste;* to the Elizabethan audience he is the familiar type of the lower-class person on the make, and expressing his upward social mobility by the clothes he wears. He is willing to cooperate with Goneril's "humour of state" so long as it promises advancement to himself; and in this he is carefully contrasted with Cornwall's servant who is never more loyal than when he tries to prevent Cornwall from tearing out Gloucester's eyes. While there is no direct suggestion of a

[2] I have made Malvolio's discourse continuous by eliminating the various interruptions of the eavesdroppers.

sexual relationship between Oswald and his mistress, something of the
same taint is produced by Goneril's willingness to have him witness
her promising Edmund her sexual favors, and by Edgar's remark after
killing him:

> I know thee well. A serviceable villain,
> As duteous to the vices of thy mistress
> As badness would desire.

The relationship between Oswald and Malvolio suggests another
important connection between the two plays, less conspicuous than
their mutual concern with clothing, but at least equally important.
That is their concern with the effect upon the social order of a belief
in Fortune's efficacy as an agent in human affairs. Here again Malvolio
provides the focus. When Maria announces the prank she will play
on Malvolio, she specifies in detail the qualities which make him an
eligible victim:

> The devil a Puritan that he is, *or anything constantly but a time-pleaser,
> an affectioned ass,* that cons state without book and utters it by great
> swarths; the best persuaded of himself; so crammed, as he thinks, with
> excellencies that it is his grounds of faith that all that look on him love
> him; and on that vice in him will my revenge find notable cause to work.

She announces her plan to her confederates; and in the great scene
where the plan is executed, she no sooner plants the forged letter and
hides herself than Malvolio comes on the stage speaking those words
above all which make him her legitimate victim: " 'Tis but fortune,
all is fortune." He reiterates almost tiresomely this belief in the su-
premacy of fortune throughout the scenes of his temptation and fall.
In his imaginary address to Sir Toby that I have quoted, he claims
that "my fortunes having cast me on your niece," he now has the
right to correct Toby's conduct. The forged letter challenges him to
be "worthy to touch Fortune's fingers." When he decides that the
letter is in earnest and his lady loves him, he says, "Jove and my stars
be praised." When he appears before his lady yellow-stockinged and
cross-gartered, he manages wholly to misconstrue Olivia's unmistakable
displeasure only because he believes that he is in friendly Fortune's
hands:

> And when she went away now, "Let this fellow be looked into." "Fel-
> low." Not "Malvolio," *nor after my degree,* but "fellow." Why, every-
> thing adheres together, that no dram of a scruple, no scruple of a scruple,
> no obstacle, no incredulous or unsafe circumstances—what can be said?
> Nothing that can be can come between me and the full prospect of my
> hopes. *Well, Jove, not I, is the doer of this, and he is to be thanked.*

Drunk with his delusion, he has forgotten what his "degree" really is. But that only leads him to believe that Olivia no longer thinks "degree" a relevant criterion of human conduct. When circumstances adhere together, degree and scruples may be forgotten. That is why only Jove is to be thanked.

Now as it is Malvolio's faith that all who look on him love him, he is like Lear at the beginning; as he is an affectioned ass, he is like Oswald; but as he is nothing constantly but a timepleaser whose goddess is Fortune, he encompasses in one stroke the whole range of evil whose separate gradations are represented in *King Lear* by Oswald, Goneril, and Edmund. A faith in the rule of capricious fortune instead of stable customs with cosmic sanctions is the central offense and villainy of both plays. And it is a familiar fact that Shakespeare attributed the belief in Fortune's supreme power specifically to his villains, from Richard III to Edmund, and that he consistently argued by his art that Fortune's devotees have room to get in the door of the social order only when degree goes out. . . .

The Fool in *Twelfth Night* is not allowed to become a "natural." And when in the guise of Sir Topas he tries to provoke Malvolio, Lear's counterpart in pride and clothes, to the same "natural" madness in which Lear outdistances his Fool, the sign of Malvolio's restoration as a man, and of his renewed adherence to custom and degree, is precisely that he does not yield to this provocation. Where Lear is chastised at the hands of Nature in the cold outdoors, Malvolio's society locks him indoors. Lear's daughters put him out with no concern for his wits one way or the other; for them his madness will be only a regrettable circumstance of Fortune. But Malvolio's tormentors try deliberately to persuade him that he is mad.

> *Malvolio.* I am not mad, Sir Topas. I say to you this house is dark.
> *Clown.* Madman, thou errest. I say there is no darkness but ignorance, in which thou art more puzzled than the Egyptians in their fog.
> *Malvolio.* I say this house is dark as ignorance, though ignorance were dark as hell; and I say there was never man thus abused. I am no more mad than you are. Make the trial of it in any constant question.
> *Clown.* What is the opinion of Pythagoras concerning wild fowl?
> *Malvolio.* That the soul of our grandam might happily inhabit a bird.
> *Clown.* What think'st thou of his opinion?
> *Malvolio.* I think nobly of the soul and no way approve his opinion.
> *Clown.* Fare thee well. Remain thou still in darkness. Thou shalt hold the opinion of Pythagoras ere I will allow of thy wits, and fear to kill a woodcock, lest thou dispossess the soul of thy grandam. Fare thee well.

Malvolio's wits are subjected to further trial before he is allowed back into the light, and they remain as clear and stable as we see them here.

The Fool's joke at the end, which deflates Pythagoras' opinion and indirectly approves Malvolio's, reassures us that Malvolio has been cured at a stroke. Malvolio's firm resistance to continued attempts to undo him into a "natural" confirms our impression that his pride has been purged, and hence reassures us that his society does not need to be dissolved. In the dialogue quoted, Malvolio's return to normality is indicated by his clarity of mind and the correctness of his philosophic manners, but most of all by his ability to participate suavely with the Fool in just the same sort of set catechism by which we have already seen the Fool mend Olivia.[3] The artful formality of the discourse signifies the health and continuity of a society which has enabled this Fool to succeed in curing Malvolio where Lear's Fool had to fail. . . .

[3] Malvolio's clarity of mind and firmness under pressure in this scene make him a less pathetic figure than he is frequently taken to be. Since his sanity remains imperturbable despite his tormentors, and since he does not indulge in self-pity, we can go on laughing at him without being altogether hard-hearted.

Twelfth Night, or What Delights You

by Clifford Leech

. . . Illyria is not everyday Elizabethan London or even the court at Whitehall. It is a land with some of its own laws, where things ripen fast, and sometimes with grace, where men are almost always at leisure for love or wine or practical jesting. Its humor, as we have noted, is less sharp than is often found in comedy: if at the end Malvolio is at odds with his fellows, they at least feel a warm desire that rancor should not be nourished.[1] Were the play all this and nothing more, it would give us much to take pleasure in. But there remains that sense of uneasy affection that the play does, I think, generally induce. To see *Twelfth Night* is to be reminded of occasions when we are making merry with those who are closest to us in sympathy and affection, and yet, though the pleasure is keen and genuine, we are fractionally conscious that the formula is not quite right, so that we cannot quite keep it from ourselves that an effort is needed for the contrivance of harmony. On such occasions the moment comes when we look coldly on the merry-making and the good relationship and see the precariousness of our tolerance for one another, the degree of pretence in all sociability. But that moment of disillusioned insight does not invalidate the experience of brief rejoicing that is possible in human encounters. There is an important sense in which any goodness in life is an artifact. Illyria, with the events it frames, is Shakespeare's image for this contrived thing: it impresses us the more deeply because from time to time Shakespeare seems deliberately to make us aware of the contrivance. The ways in which he does this will be my concern in the remainder of this lecture.

And first, of course, there is the problem of Malvolio. Lamb says: "I confess that I never saw the catastrophe of this character, while Bensley played it, without a kind of tragic interest." [2] But in saying

---

[1] Feste should be excepted. See p. 45.

[2] *Essays of Elia* (World's Classics, 1901, reprinted 1903), p. 189.

that, Lamb has rather bedevilled the issue. We are not concerned with tragedy in *Twelfth Night*. "Tragedy" implies a whole view of the universe, in which man's sureness of defeat is seen at odds with his magnitude of spirit. The dominant attitude of *Twelfth Night* is far from that: the play is concerned, rather, with man's subjection to a relatively kindly puppet-master, and Malvolio, however he may suffer, is not a symbol of human greatness. If we are to look for a resemblance between him and other Shakespearian characters, we shall find his kin not among the tragic heroes but rather in the Parolles of *All's Well that Ends Well*. Parolles is a braggart and a coward, who is finally exposed when he shows himself willing to buy his life with treachery. The world of *All's Well* is much darker than that of *Twelfth Night*, and fittingly, therefore, Parolles' failings are deeper than Malvolio's. But their resemblance lies in our response to their humiliation. Both of them become aware of solitude. When that happens to Parolles, he shows an interesting resilience: "Even the thing I am shall make me live," he says, and he is willing to accept the scorn of men who are safe in their noble station, if they will, nevertheless, find a place in their charity for him. Malvolio shows not resilience but a sense of outrage. "Madam, you have done me wrong, notorious wrong" is his cry to Olivia when he is brought from the darkness of his cell to the bright end of the comedy, and his final words, "I'll be revenged on the whole pack of you," leave us uneasy at the gull's intransigence and wincing at the word "pack." Thus he becomes a stronger, more independent figure than Parolles, but they are alike in our sense of discomfort in their baiting. Illyria, like the France and Italy of *All's Well*, cannot exist without a strain of cruelty, of persecution. We cannot have our Illyria, in fact, without an echo of the common world. Even Sir Toby, who has been a prime mover in the gulling of Malvolio, confesses he is uneasy about what has been done:

I would we were well rid of this knavery. If he may be conveniently delivered, I would he were, for I am now so far in offence with my niece, that I cannot pursue with any safety this sport to the upshot.

(IV.ii.72-77)

And Olivia and the Duke, the persons of authority in this play's world, are anxious that all shall be put right. Yet it is apparent that it cannot be put right. The humiliation of Malvolio is the price that one pays for practical jesting: one cannot strip the self-important and the puritanical without sharing their embarrassment at nakedness. To put Malvolio on a tragic level is to disregard the general effect of his appearance on the stage: rather, he is one of those comic figures at whom it is too easy to laugh, so easy that, before we know it, we have done harm and are ashamed. At the end of *All's Well* we may feel more in sympathy with Parolles than with any other character. That is not the case with Malvolio and *Twelfth Night,* for the dominant mood of this comedy is gentler and we are here more closely in tune with the denouement.

Yet even in this relaxed comedy, with its conclusion in Viola's victory over Orsino's heart and Olivia's winning at least the appearance of the man she had fallen in love with, we are not long allowed to forget the harshness of things. Malvolio is suddenly brought to Olivia's mind in the last scene because Viola mentions the imprisonment "at Malvolio's suit" of the captain who had helped her when she arrived in Illyria. It is evident that the ambitious steward has exercised authority with a long arm: our realization of that moderates our pity for him. Then, when "the madly us'd Malvolio" is brought onstage, and the whole story is told, Feste runs through the matter of the gulling, with a special sourness in recalling how Malvolio had spoken contemptuously of him at the beginning of the play. Audiences in the Neptune Theatre will I think be conscious of the sharp and emphatic way in which this production's Feste, Mr. David Renton, delivered these lines:

> Why, "some are born great, some achieve greatness, and some have greatness thrown upon them." I was one, sir, in this interlude—one Sir Topas, sir; but that's all one. "By the Lord, fool, I am not mad!" But do you remember—"Madam, why laugh you at such a barren rascal? An you smile not, he's gagg'd?" And thus the whirligig of time brings in his revenges.

> (V.i.378-385)

It is hard to be reminded of one's own words, especially at the moment of humiliation, and Feste's remorselessness here, while not putting us on Malvolio's side, makes us realize what it is like to be in his situation. The "whiligig of time" only for a moment appears to be a light-hearted and irreverent way of referring to Fortune's wheel: the fun evaporates with the word "revenges." This is a vindictive Fortune, a Fortune who not only turns her wheel but punishes. Her spokesman is the clever and engaging Fool.

Against Fortune, against the general laughter of Orsino's and Olivia's people, there stands the mock-madman madly used, the petty tyrant who now in his turn talks of revenge. We are made conscious that this despised man, the man outside the orbit of harmony, makes, almost like Gregers Werle in Ibsen's *The Wild Duck,* his "demand of the ideal." We feel, like Olivia and the Duke, the pity of life's refusal even in this comedy to sort itself out with a uniformity of happiness. The play is the stronger for its sense of this impossibility.

There are other traces of human suffering in this play. Antonio's

relation with Sebastian has its poignancy. On his first appearance he
tells Sebastian of the danger he runs in coming near Orsino's court,
but he is willing to risk that to be near his friend. His language here
is curiously emphatic:

> I have many enemies in Orsino's court,
> Else would I very shortly see thee there.
> But come what may, I do adore thee so
> That danger shall seem sport, and I will go.
>
> (II.i.46-49)

"Adore" is a strong word in Shakespeare. It prepares us for Antonio's
violence of language when he believes that Sebastian has betrayed
him in his time of necessity:

> *Ant.* Let me speak a little. This youth that you see here
> I snatch'd one half out of the jaws of death,
> Reliev'd him with such sanctity of love,
> And to his image, which methought did promise
> Most venerable worth, did I devotion.
> *1 Off.* What's that to us? The time goes by; away.
> *Ant.* But, O, how vile an idol proves this god!
> Thou hast, Sebastian, done good feature shame.
> In nature there's no blemish but the mind:
> None can be call'd deform'd but the unkind.
> Virtue is beauty; but the beauteous evil
> Are empty trunks, o'erflourish'd by the devil.
> *1 Off.* The man grows mad. Away with him.
>
> (III.iv.393-405)

And in the last scene of the comedy he speaks at length of his "love"
and of the ingratitude it has met with:

> A witchcraft drew me hither:
> That most ingrateful boy there by your side
> From the rude sea's enrag'd and foamy mouth
> Did I redeem; a wreck past hope he was.
> His life I gave him, and did thereto add
> My love without retention or restraint,
> All his in dedication; for his sake,
> Did I expose myself, pure for his love,
> Into the danger of this adverse town;
> Drew to defend him when he was beset;
> Where being apprehended, his false cunning,
> Not meaning to partake with me in danger,
> Taught him to face me out of his acquaintance,

> And grew a twenty years removed thing
> While one could wink.
>
> (V.i.79-93)

Immediately afterwards Orsino is reproaching the disguised Viola in similar terms, thinking that the boy he has befriended has shown a perfidy like that which Antonio has believed himself to find in Sebastian: the parallelism is comic and prevents us from taking Antonio's plight overseriously for more than a moment. Yet for that moment he brings to us a strong sense of disillusioned friendship. If we compare it with Valentine's disappointment with Proteus in *The Two Gentlemen of Verona*, we see that here Shakespeare has much more fully imagined the situation. And while Antonio remains on the stage, we have before us a reminder that humanity is vulnerable through its attachments, that affection puts a man in another's power. . . .

Twelfth Night and the Morality of Indulgence

by John Hollander

To say that a play is "moral" would seem to imply that it represents
an action which concretizes certain ethical elements of human experience, without actually moralizing at any point, and without having
any of the characters in it state univocally a dogma, precept, or value
that would coincide completely with the play's own moral intention.
It was just this univocal didacticism, however, which characterized
what was becoming in 1600 a prevailing comic tradition. The moral
intent of the Jonsonian "comedy of humours" was direct and didactic; its purpose was to show

> the times deformitie
> Anatomiz'd in euery nerue and sinnew
> With constant courage, and contempt of feare.[1]

For moral purposes, a humour is an identifying emblem of a man's
moral nature, graven ineradicably onto his physiological one. In the
world of a play, a humour could be caricatured to such a degree that
it would practically predestine a character's behavior. It was made to

> . . . so possesse a man, that it doth draw
> All his affects, his spirits and his powers,
> In their confluctions, all to runne one way,
> This may be truly said to be a Humour.

The emblematic character of the humour, and the necessity for its use,
were affirmed even more directly by Sidney, whose dramatic theory
Jonson seems to have greatly admired:

> Now, as in Geometry the oblique must bee knowne as wel as the right,
> and in Arithmeticke the odde as well as the euen, so in the actions of

"Twelfth Night and the Morality of Indulgence" by John Hollander. From The
Sewanee Review, LXVIII (1959), 220-238. Copyright © 1959 by the University of
the South. Reprinted by permission of John Hollander and The Sewanee Review.

[1] Ben Jonson, *Every Man Out of His Humour* (1599), Induction, II. 120-122.

our life who seeth not the filthiness of euil wanteth a great foile to per-
ceiue the beauty of vertue. This doth the Comedy handle so in our
priuate and domestical matters, as with hearing it we get as it were an
experience, what is to be looked for of a nigardly *Demea*, of a crafty
Dauus, of a flattering *Gnato*, of a vaine glorious *Thraso*, and not onely
to know what effects are to be expected, but to know who be such, by the
signifying badge giuen them by the Comedian.

Now *Every Man In His Humour* was first acted in 1598, and it is
known that Shakespeare appeared in it. He seems in *Twelfth Night*
(for which I accept the traditional date of 1600-1601) to have at-
tempted to write a kind of moral comedy diametrically opposed to
that of Jonson, in which "the times deformitie" was not to be "anato-
miz'd," but represented in the core of an action. For a static and
deterministic Humour, Shakespeare substituted a kinetic, governing
Appetite in the action, rather than in the bowels, of his major characters. In his plot and language, he insists continually on the fact and
importance of the substitution. Characters in a comedy of humours
tend to become caricatures, and caricatures tend to become beasts,
inhuman personifications of moral distortions that are identified with
physiological ones. I believe that it was Shakespeare's intention in
Twelfth Night to obviate the necessity of this dehumanization by substituting what one might call a moral process for a moral system.
While it is true that the play contains quite a bit of interesting discussion of humours as such, and that there is some correspondence between appetites and humours, it is equally true that the only person
in the play who believes in the validity of humourous classifications,
who, indeed, lives by them, is himself a moral invalid. I will have
more to say about this later. At this point I merely wish to suggest
that the primary effective difference between Shakespeare's and Jonson's techniques in making moral comedy is the difference between
what is merely a display of anatomy, and a dramatization of a metaphor, the difference between a Pageant and an Action.

II

The Action of *Twelfth Night* is indeed that of a Revels, a suspension of mundane affairs during a brief epoch in a temporary world
of indulgence, a land full of food, drink, love, play, disguise and music. But parties end, and the reveller eventually becomes satiated and
drops heavily into his worldly self again. The fact that plays were
categorized as "revells" for institutional purposes may have appealed
to Shakespeare; he seems at any rate to have analyzed the dramatic

and moral nature of feasting, and to have made it the subject of his play. His analysis is schematized in Orsino's opening speech.

The essential action of a revels is: To so surfeit the Appetite upon excess that it "may sicken and so die." It is the Appetite, not the whole Self, however, which is surfeited: the Self will emerge at the conclusion of the action from where it has been hidden. The movement of the play is toward this emergence of humanity from behind a mask of comic type.

Act I, Scene 1, is very important as a statement of the nature of this movement. Orsino's opening line contains the play's three dominant images:

> If music be the food of love, play on.
> Give me excess of it, that, surfeiting,
> The appetite may sicken, and so die.   (I.i.1-3)

Love, eating, and music are the components of the revelry, then. And in order that there be no mistake about the meaning of the action, we get a miniature rehearsal of it following immediately:

> That strain again! It had a dying fall.
> Oh, it came o'er my ear like the sweet sound
> That breathes upon a bank of violets
> Stealing and giving odor! Enough, no more.
> 'Tis not so sweet now as it was before.
> O spirit of love, how quick and fresh art thou!
> That, notwithstanding thy capacity
> Receiveth as the sea, naught enters there,
> Of what validity and pitch soe'er,
> But falls into abatement and low price,
> Even in a minute! So full of shapes is fancy
> That it alone is high fantastical.   (I.i.4-15)

A bit of surfeiting is actually accomplished here; what we are getting is a proem to the whole play, and a brief treatment of love as an appetite. The substance of a feast will always fall into "abatement and low price" at the conclusion of the feasting, for no appetite remains to demand it. We also think of Viola in connection with the "violets/ Stealing and giving odor," for her actual position as go-between-turned-lover is one of both inadvertent thief and giver. The Duke's rhetoric is all-embracing, however, and he immediately comments significantly upon his own condition.

> Oh, when mine eyes did see Olivia first,
> Methought she purged the air of pestilence!

> That instant was I turned into a hart,
> And my desires, like fell and cruel hounds,
> E'er since pursue me.   (I.i.19-23)

Like Actaeon, he is the hunter hunted; the active desirer pursued by his own desires. As embodying this overpowering appetite for romantic love, he serves as a host of the revels.[2]

The other host is Olivia, the subject of his desire. We see almost at once that her self-indulgence is almost too big to be encompassed by Orsino's. Valentine, reporting on the failure of his mission, describes her state as follows:

> So please my lord, I might not be admitted,
> But from her handmaid do return this answer:
> The element itself, till seven years' heat,
> Shall not behold her face at ample view;
> But, like a cloistress, she will veiled walk
> And water once a day her chamber round
> With eye-offending brine—all this to season
> A brother's dead love, which she would keep fresh
> And lasting in her sad remembrance.   (I.i.24-32)

"To season a brother's dead love": she is gorging herself on this fragrant herb, and though she has denied herself the world, she is no true anchorite, but, despite herself, a private glutton. The Duke looks forward to the end of her feast of grief,

> . . . when liver, brain, and heart,
> These sovereign thrones, are all supplied, and filled
> Her sweet perfections with one self king!   (I.i.37-39)

The trinitarian overtone is no blasphemy, but a statement of the play's teleology. When everyone is supplied with "one self king," the action will have been completed.

The first three scenes of the play stand together as a general prologue, in which the major characters are introduced and their active natures noted. Viola is juxtaposed to Olivia here; she is not one to drown her own life in a travesty of mourning. It is true that she is tempted to "serve that lady" (as indeed she does, in a different way). But her end in so doing would be the whole play's action in microcosm; the immersion in committed self-indulgence would result in the revelation of her self:

[2] See the extremely provocative commentary on the Duke's opening lines in Kenneth Burke, *The Philosophy of Literary Form* (Baton Rouge, 1941), pp. 344-349.

> And might not be delivered to the world
> Till I had made mine own occasion mellow,
> What my estate is.   (I.ii.42-44)

She will serve the Duke instead, and use her persuasive talents to accomplish the ends to which his own self-celebrating rhetoric can provide no access. "I can sing," she says, "and speak to him in many sorts of music." Her sense of his character has been verified; the Captain tells her that his name is as his nature. And "what is his name?" she asks. "Orsino," answers the Captain. Orsino—the bear, the ravenous and clumsy devourer. Her own name suggests active, affective music; and the mention of Arion, the Orpheus-like enchanter of waves and dolphins with his music, points up the connotation. Orsino's "music," on the other hand, is a static well of emotion to which he allows his own rhetoric to submerge; Viola's is more essentially instrumental, effective, and convincing.[3]

The third scene of Act I completes the prologue by further equating the moral and physiological. Here we first encounter the world of what Malvolio calls "Sir Toby and the lighter people" (it is indeed true that there is none of Malvolio's element of "earth" in them). The continued joking about *dryness* that pervades the wit here in Olivia's house, both above and below stairs, is introduced here, in contrast to Olivia's floods of welling and self-indulgent tears. The idea behind the joking in this and the followng scenes is that drinking and merriment will moisten and fulfill a dry nature. As Feste says later on, "Give the dry fool drink, then the fool is not dry." Toby's sanguine temperament and Aguecheek's somewhat phlegmatic one are here unveiled. They are never identified as such, however; and none of the wit that is turned on the associations of "humours," "elements," and "waters," though it runs throughout the play, ever refers to a motivating order in the universe, except insofar as Malvolio believes in it.

What is most important is that neither Feste, the feaster embodying not the spirit but the action of revelry, nor Malvolio, the ill-wisher (and the *bad appetite* as well), his polar opposite, appears in these introductory scenes. It is only upstairs in Olivia's house (I,v) that the action as such commences. The revels opens with Feste's exchange with Maria in which she attempts three times to insist on innocent interpretations of "well-hanged" and "points." But Feste is resolute in his ribaldry. Thus Olivia, momentarily voicing Malvolio's

---

[3] See my own "Musica Mundana and Twelfth Night" in *Sound and Poetry,* ed. Northrop Frye (New York, 1957) , pp. 55-82, for an extended treatment of the use of "speculative" and "practical" music in the play.

invariable position, calls Feste a "dry fool," and "dishonest"; Malvolio himself refers to him as a "barren rascal." From here on in it will
be Feste who dances attendance on the revelry, singing, matching wit
with Viola, and being paid by almost everyone for his presence. To
a certain degree he remains outside the action, not participating in
it because he represents its very nature; occasionally serving as a comic
angel or messenger, he is nevertheless unmotivated by any appetite,
and is never sated of his fooling. His insights into the action are continuous, and his every remark is telling. "*Cucullus non facit mon-
achum*. That's as much as to say I wear not motley in my brain." [4]
Indeed, he does not, but more important is the fact that his robe and
beard are not to make him a *real* priest later on. And neither he as
Sir Thopas, nor Olivia as a "cloistress," nor Malvolio in his black
suit or travestied virtue, nor the transvestite Viola is what he appears
to be. No one will be revealed in his true dress until he has doffed his
mask of feasting. And although neither Feste nor Malvolio will change
in this respect, it is for completely opposite reasons that they will not
do so.

Every character in the play, however, is granted some degree of insight into the nature of the others. It is almost as if everyone were
masked with the black side of his vizard turned inwards; he sees more
clearly past the *persona* of another than he can past his own. Valentine, for the Duke, comments on Olivia, as we have seen before. Even
Malvolio is granted such an insight. Olivia asks him "What manner
of man" Caesario is; unwittingly, his carping, over self-conscious and
intellectualized answer cuts straight to the heart of Viola's disguise:
"Not yet old enough for a man, nor young enough for a boy, as a
squash is before 'tis a peascod, or a codling when 'tis almost an apple.
'Tis with him in standing water, between boy and man. He is very
well-favored and he speaks very shrewishly. One would think his
mother's milk were scarce out of him" (I.v.165-171).

The puns on "cod" and "codling" insist on being heard here, and
as with the inadvertently delivered obscenity about Olivia's "great
P's" and their source in the letter scene, Malvolio does not know what
he is saying. The point is that Malvolio asserts, for an audience that
knows the real facts, that Viola can scarcely be a male creature.

A more significant case of this hide-and-seek is Olivia's retort to
Malvolio in the same scene: "O you are sick of self-love, Malvolio, and
taste with a distempered appetite"; it provides the key to his physio-
logical-moral nature. "Sick of self-love" means "sick with a moral in-
fection called self-love," but it can also mean "already surfeited, or
fed up with your own ego as an object of appetite." Malvolio's "dis-

---

[4] Cf. *Measure for Measure* (V.i.263), where Lucio refers in the identical words to
the Duke disguised as Friar Lodowick.

tempered appetite" results from the fact that he alone is not possessed of a craving directed outward, towards some object on which it can surfeit and die; he alone cannot morally benefit from a period of self-indulgence. Actually this distemper manifests itself in terms of transitory desires on his part for status and for virtue, but these desires consume him in their fruitlessness; he is aware of the nature of neither of them. This is a brilliant analysis of the character of a melancholic, and Shakespeare's association of the melancholy, puritanic, and status-seeking characters in Malvolio throws considerable light on all of them. The moral nature of the plot of *Twelfth Night* can be easily approached through the character of Malvolio, and this, I think, is what Lamb and his followers missed completely in their egalitarian sympathy for his being no "more than steward." For Malvolio's attachment to self-advancement is not being either aristocratically ridiculed or praised as an example of righteous bourgeois opposition to medieval hierarchies. In the context of the play's moral physiology, his disease is shown forth as a case of indigestion due to his self-love, the result of a perverted, rather than an excessive appetite.[5] In the world of feasting, the values of the commercial society outside the walls of the party go topsy-turvy: Feste is given money for making verbal fools of the donors thereof; everyone's desire is fulfilled in an unexpected way; and revellers are shown to rise through realms of unreality, disguise, and luxurious self-deception. We are seduced, by the revelling, away from seeing the malice in the plot to undo Malvolio. But whatever malice there is remains peculiarly just. It is only Malvolio who bears any ill will, and only he upon whom ill will can appear to be directed. He makes for himself a hell of the worldly heaven of festivity, and when Toby and Maria put him into darkness, into a counterfeit hell, they are merely representing in play a condition that he has already achieved.

The plot against Malvolio, then, is no more than an attempt to let him surfeit on himself, to present him with those self-centered, "time-pleasing" objects upon which his appetite is fixed. In essence, he is led to a feast in which his own vision of himself is spread before him, and commanded to eat it. The puritan concern with witchcraft and the satanic, and its associations of them with madness are carried to a logical extreme; and once Malvolio has been permitted to indulge in his self-interest by means of the letter episode, he is only treated as he would himself treat anyone whom he believed to be mad. His puritanism is mocked by allusions to his praying made by Toby and Maria; a priest (and a false, dissembling one at that, the answer to a

---

[5] And Leslie Hotson has pointed out that his yellow stockings, as he later appears in them, are the true color of the Narcissus, as well as of the craven. See *The First Night of Twelfth Night* (London, 1954), p. 98f.

puritan's prayer) is sent to him; and the implications of the darkness
are eventually fulfilled as his prison becomes his hell.

It is interesting to notice how carefully Shakespeare analyzed another characteristic of the melancholic in his treatment of Malvolio.
L. C. Knights has suggested [6] that the vogue of melancholy at the
turn of the seventeenth century was occasioned to some degree by the
actual presence in England of a large number of *"intellectuels en
chômage"* (in Denis de Rougement's words), unemployed, university-
trained men whose humanistic education had not fitted them for any
suitable role in society. Malvolio is no patent and transparent university intellectual (like Holofernes, for example). He contrives, however, to over-rationalize his point (where the Duke will over-senti-
mentalize it) on almost every occasion. Even his first introduction of
Viola, as has been seen before, is archly over-reasoned. His venture
into exegesis of a text is almost telling.

It is not merely self-interest, I think, that colors the scrutiny of
Maria's letter. His reading is indeed a close one: he observes that,
after the first snatch of doggerel, "The numbers altered." But Malvolio
is incapable of playing the party-game and guessing the riddle. Of
"M,O,A,I doth sway my life," he can only say "And yet to crush
this a little it would bow to me, for every one of these letters are in
my name." He even avoids the reading that should, by all rights, appeal to him: Leslie Hotson has suggested that "M,O,A,I" probably
stands for *Mare, Orbis, Aer,* and *Ignis,* the four elements to which
Malvolio so often refers. Malvolio himself fails as a critic, following
a "cold scent" that, as Fabian indicates, is "as rank as a fox" for him
in that it tantalizes his ambition.

But he continues to aspire to scholarship. In order to let his tongue
tang with arguments of state, he intends to "read politic authors." His
intrusion on the scene of Toby's and Andrew's merry-making involves a most significant remark: "Is there no respect of persons, time,
or place in you?", he asks. In other words, "Do you not observe even
the dramatic unities in your revelling? Can you not apply even the
values that govern things as frivolous as plays to your lives?" Coming from Malvolio, the ethical theorist, the remark feels very different
from the remark made to Sir Toby by Maria, the practical moralist:
"Aye, but you must confine yourself within the modest levels of order."
Maria, presiding over the festivities, would keep things from getting
out of hand. It is not only the spirit in which Malvolio's comment is
uttered that accounts for this difference, however. I think that one
of the implications is quite clearly the fact that Jonson's ordered,
would-be-classic, but static and didactic comedy would disapprove of

---

[6] *Drama and Society in the Age of Jonson* (Manchester, 1936), pp. 315-332.

Twelfth Night as a moral play, and mistake its intention for a purely frivolous one.

The prank played on Malvolio is not merely an "interwoven" second story, but a fully developed double-plot. Like the Belmont episodes in *The Merchant of Venice*, it is a condensed representation of the action of the entire play. In *Twelfth Night*, however, it operates in reverse, to show the other side of the coin, as it were. For Malvolio there can be no fulfillment in "one self king." His story effectively and ironically underlines the progress toward this fulfillment in everybody else, and helps to delineate the limitations of the moral domain of the whole play. In contrast to Feste, who appears in the action at times as an abstracted spirit of revelry, Malvolio is a model of the sinner.

The whole play abounds in such contrasts and parallels of character, and the players form and regroup continually with respect to these, much in the manner of changing figurations in a suite of *branles*. Viola herself indulges in the festivities in a most delicate and (literally) charming way. She is almost too good a musician, too effective an Orpheus: "Heaven forbid my outside have not charmed her," she complains after her first encounter with Olivia. But as soon as she realizes that she is part of the game, she commits herself to it with redoubled force. If her "outside" is directed toward Olivia, her real identity and her own will are concentrated even more strongly on Orsino. In the most ironic of the love scenes she all but supplants Olivia in the Duke's affections. Orsino, glutting himself on his own version of romantic love, allows himself to make the most extravagant and self-deceptive statements about it:

> Come hither, boy. If ever thou shalt love,
> In the sweet pangs of it remember me;
> For such as I am all true lovers are,
> Unstaid and skittish in all motions else
> Save in the constant image of the creature
> That is beloved. (II.iv.15-20)

This skittishness, beneath the mask of the ravenous and constant bear, is obvious to Feste at least: "Now, the melancholy god protect thee, and the tailor make thy doublet of changeable taffeta, for thy mind is a very opal. I would have men of such constancy put to sea, that their business might be everything and their intent everywhere; for that's it that always makes a good voyage of nothing." (II.iv.75-80)

Orsino also gives us a curious version of the physiology of the passions on which the plot is based; it is only relatively accurate, of course, for he will be the last of the revellers to feel stuffed, to push away from him his heaping dish.

> There is no woman's sides
> Can bide the beating of so strong a passion
> As love doth give my heart, no woman's heart
> So big to hold so much. They lack retention.
> Alas, their love may be called appetite—
> No motion of the liver, but the palate—
> They suffer surfeit, cloyment and revolt.
> But mine is all as hungry as the sea
> And can digest as much.   (II.iv.96-104)

Viola has been giving him her "inside" throughout the scene, and were he not still ravenous for Olivia's love he could see her for what she is: a woman with a constancy in love (for himself and her brother) that he can only imagine himself to possess. She is indeed an Allegory of Patience on some baroque tomb at this point. She is ironically distinguished from Olivia in that her "smiling at grief" is a disguising "outside" for her real sorrow, whereas Olivia's is a real self-indulgent pleasure taken at a grief outworn. It is as if Olivia had misread Scripture and taken the letter of "Blessed are they that mourn" for the spirit of it. Her grief is purely ceremonial.

The "lighter people," too, are engaged in carrying out the action in their own way, and they have more business in the play than merely to make a gull of Malvolio. Toby's huge stomach for food and drink parallels the Duke's ravenous capacity for sentiment. The drinking scene is in one sense the heart of the play. It starts out by declaring itself in no uncertain terms. "Does not our life consist of the four elements?" catechizes Sir Toby. "Faith, so they say," replies Andrew, "but I think it rather consists of eating and drinking." No one but Feste, perhaps, really knows the extent to which this is true, for Andrew is actually saying "We are not merely comic types, mind you, being manipulated by a dramatist of the humours. The essence of our lives lies in a movement from hunger to satiety that we share with all of nature."

When Toby and Andrew cry out for a love song, Feste obliges them, not with the raucous bawdy thing that one would expect, but instead, with a direct appeal to their actual hostess, Olivia. This is all the more remarkable in that it is made on behalf of everyone in the play. "O Mistress Mine" undercuts the Duke's overwhelming but ineffectual mouthings, Viola's effective but necessarily misdirected charming, and, of course, Aguecheek's absolute incompetence as a suitor. The argument is couched in purely naturalistic terms: "This feast will have to end, and so will all of our lives. You are not getting younger ('sweet and twenty' is the contemporaneous equivalent of 'sweet and thirty,' at least). Give up this inconstant roaming; your little game had better end in your marriage, anyway." The true love "that can sing both high and low" is Viola-Sebastian, the master-mistress of Orsino's and Olivia's passion. (Sebastian has just been introduced in the previous scene, and there are overtones here of his being invoked as Olivia's husband). Sebastian has, aside from a certain decorative but benign courtly manner, no real identity apart from Viola. He is the fulfillment of her longing (for she has thought him dead) and the transformation into reality of the part she is playing in the *ludus amoris.* The prognostication is borne out by Sebastian's own remark: "You are betrothed both to a man and maid." He is himself characterized by an elegance hardly virile; and, finally, we must keep in mind the fact that Viola was played by a boy actor to begin with, and that Shakespeare's audience seemed to be always ready for an intricate irony of this kind.

But if Viola and Sebastian are really the same, "One face, one voice, one habit, and two persons, A natural perspective that is and is not," there is an interesting parallel between Viola and Aguecheek as well. Both are suitors for Olivia's hand: Andrew, ineffectively, for himself; Viola for Orsino, and (effectively) for Sebastian. Their confrontation in the arranged duel is all the more ironic in that Andrew is an effective pawn in Toby's game (Toby is swindling him), whereas Viola is an ineffective one in the Duke's (she is swindling him of Olivia's love).

Feste's other songs differ radically from "O Mistress Mine." He sings for the Duke a kind of languorous ayre, similar to so many that one finds in the songbooks.[7] It is aimed at Orsino in the very extravagance of its complaint. It is his own song, really, if we imagine him suddenly dying of love, being just as ceremoniously elaborate in his funeral instructions as he has been in his suit of Olivia. And Feste's bit of handy-dandy to Malvolio in his prison is a rough-and-tumble sort of thing, intended to suggest in its measures a scrap from a Morality, plainly invoking Malvolio in darkness as a devil in hell. Feste shows himself throughout the play to be a master of every convention of fooling.

If Feste's purpose is to serve as a symbol of the revels, however, he must also take a clear and necessary part in the all-important conclusion. *Twelfth Night* itself, the feast of the Epiphany, celebrates the discovery of the "True King" in the manger by the Wise Men. "Those wits," says Feste in Act I, Scene 5 "that think they have thee [wit] do very oft prove fools, and I that am sure I lack thee may pass for a wise man." And so it is that under his influence the true Caesario,

---

[7] The Rev. E. H. Fellowes, in *English Madrigal Verse* (Oxford, 1929), lists four different ayres with the conventional opening phrase, "Come away."

the "one self king," is revealed.[8] The whole of Act V might be taken, in connection with "the plot" in a trivial sense, to be the other *epiphany,* the perception that follows the *anagnorisis* or discovery of classic dramaturgy. But we have been dealing with the Action of *Twelfth Night* as representing the killing off of excessive appetite through indulgence of it, leading to the rebirth of the unencumbered self. The long final scene, then, serves to show forth the Caesario-King, and to unmask, discover, and reveal the fulfilled selves in the major characters.

The appearance of the priest (a real one, this time) serves more than the simple purpose of proving the existence of a marriage between Olivia and "Caesario." It is a simple but firm intrusion into the world of the play of a way of life that has remained outside of it so far. The straightforward solemnity of the priest's rhetoric is also something new; suggestions of its undivided purpose have appeared before only in Antonio's speeches. The priest declares that Olivia and her husband have been properly married:

> And all the ceremony of this compact
> Sealed in my function, by my testimony.
> Since when, my watch hath told me, toward my grave
> I have travelled but two hours.   (V.i.163-166)

It is possible that the original performances had actually taken about two hours to reach this point. At any rate, the sombre acknowledgment of the passage of time in a real world is there. Antonio has prepared the way earlier in the scene; his straightforward confusion is that of the unwitting intruder in a masquerade who has been accused of mistaking the identities of two of the masquers.

That the surfeiting has gradually begun to occur, however, has become evident earlier. In the prison scene, Sir Toby has already begun to tire: "I would we were well rid of this knavery." He gives as his excuse for this the fact that he is already in enough trouble with Olivia, but such as this has not deterred him in the past. And, in the last scene, very drunk as he must be, he replies to Orsino's inquiry as to his condition that he hates the surgeon, "a drunken rogue." Self-knowledge has touched Sir Toby. He could not have said this earlier.

As the scene plays itself out, Malvolio alone is left unaccounted for. There is no accounting for him here, though; he remains a bad taste in the mouth. "Alas poor fool," says Olivia, "How have they baffled thee!" And thus, in Feste's words, "the whirligig of time brings in his revenges." Malvolio has become the fool, the "barren rascal." He

---

[8] For my interpretation of the last act I am indebted to Professor Roy W. Battenhouse's suggestions.

leaves in a frenzy, to "be revenged," he shouts, "on the whole pack of you." He departs from the world of this play to resume a role in another, perhaps. His reincarnation might be as Middleton's De Flores, rather than even Jaques. His business has never been with the feasting to begin with, and now that it is over, and the revellers normalized, he is revealed as the true madman. He is "The Madly-Used Malvolio" to the additional degree that his own uses have been madness.

For Orsino and Viola the end has also arrived. She will be "Orsino's mistress and his fancy's queen." He has been surfeited of his misdirected voracity; the rich golden shaft, in his own words, "hath killed the flock of all affections else" that live in him. "Liver, brain and heart" are indeed all supplied; for both Olivia and himself, there has been fulfillment in "one self king." And, lest there be no mistake, each is to be married to a Caesario or king. Again, "Liver, brain and heart" seems to encompass everybody: Toby and Maria are married, Aguecheek chastened, etc.

At the end of the scene, all exit. Only Feste, the pure fact of feasting, remains. His final song is a summation of the play in many ways at once. Its formal structure seems to be a kind of quick rehearsal of the Ages of Man. In youth, "A foolish thing was but a toy": the fool's bauble, emblematic of both his *membrum virile* and his trickery, is a trivial fancy. But in "man's estate," the bauble represents a threat of knavery and thievery to respectable society, who shuts its owner out of doors. The "swaggering" and incessant drunkenness of the following strophes bring Man into prime and dotage, respectively. Lechery, trickery, dissembling, and drunkenness, inevitable and desperate in mundane existence, however, are just those activities which, mingled together in a world of feasting, serve to purge Man of the desire for them. The wind and the rain accompany him throughout his life, keeping him indoors with "dreams and imaginations" as a boy, pounding and drenching him unmercifully, when he is locked out of doors, remaining eternal and inevitable throughout his pride in desiring to perpetuate himself. The wind and the rain are the most desperate of elements, that pound the walls and batter the roof of the warm house that shuts them out, while, inside it, the revels are in progress. Only after the party is ended can Man face them without desperation.

It is the metaphor of the rain that lasts longest, though, and it recapitulates the images of water, elements and humours that have pervaded the entire play. Feste himself, who tires of nothing, addresses Viola: "Who you are and what you would are out of my welkin —I might say 'element' but the word is overworn." He adroitly comments on Malvolio's line "Go to; I am not of your element" by substituting a Saxon word for a Latin one. The additional association of the four elements with the humours cannot be overlooked. It is only Malvolio, of course, who uses the word "humour" with any seriousness: "And then to have the humour of State," he muses, as he imagines himself "Count Malvolio." Humours are also waters, however. And *waters*, or fluids of all kinds, are continually being forced on our attention. Wine, tears, seawater, even urine, are in evidence from the first scene on, and they are always being metaphorically identified with one another. They are all fluids, bathing the world of the play in possibilities for change as the humours do the body. Feste's answer to Maria in the prison scene has puzzled many editors; if we realize, however, that Feste is probably hysterically laughing at what he has just been up to, "Nay, I'm for all waters" may have the additional meaning that he is on the verge of losing control of himself. He is "for all waters" primarily in that he represents the fluidity of revelling celebration. And finally, when all is done, "The rain it raineth every day," and Feste reverts to gnomic utterance in a full and final seriousness. Water is rain that falls to us from Heaven. The world goes on. Our revels now are ended, but the actors solidify into humanity, in this case. "But that's all one, our play is done/And we'll strive to please you every day."

III

In this interpretation of *Twelfth Night,* I have in no sense meant to infer that Malvolio is to be identified as Ben Jonson, or that the play functioned in any systematic way in the war of the theatres. There are, of course, a number of propitious coincidences: Marston's *What You Will,* coming some six or seven years after *Twelfth Night,* devotes much effort to lampooning Jonson. What could have been meant by the title, however, as well as Shakespeare's real intention in his subtitle, remains obscure. Perhaps they both remain as the first part of some forgotten proverb to the effect that what you will (want) may come to you in an unexpected form. Perhaps they are both merely throwaway comments to the effect that the play is really "what you may call it." (It has been frequently suggested that it is a translation of Rabelais' *"Fay ce que vouldras."*) Then there is the dig, in *Every Man Out of His Humour,* at a comedy with a romantic (Italianate) plot more than vaguely resembling that of *Twelfth Night. Every Man Out* has been dated in 1599, but the idea that Shakespeare may have chosen just such a "romantic" story with which to oppose Jonson's comic theories is not inconceivable.

My point, however, is that *Twelfth Night* is opposed by its very nature to the kind of comedy that Jonson was not only writing, but advocating at the time; that is a moral comedy, representing human experience in terms of a fully dramatized metaphor rather than a static emblematic correspondence; and, finally, that it operates to refute the moral validity of comedy of humours in its insistence on the active metaphor of surfeiting the appetite, upon which the whole plot is constructed. It is only romantic in that it shares, with *As You Like It* (and with *Love's Labours Lost*, too, for that matter) a hint of the world of transformation of the last plays. Its moral vision is as intense as that of the problem comedies.

The Consummation

by H. B. Charlton

. . . So, amongst the themes of Elizabethan comedy, love had now justified its primacy. It had willy-nilly always been the major interest. But, as the earlier comedies have shown, its usurpations had been hazardous for the spirit of comedy. It had hitherto forced itself into a Pyrrhic triumph as an alien invader backed only by the forces of popular preference. It could now rightly take its place in Elizabethan comedy as the recognised presiding genius. It was the touchstone by which fine spirits were struck to their finest issues. It was also, of course, a test by which weaker mortals revealed their weakness, grosser ones their grossness, and foolish ones their folly. It is noteworthy, however, that though these three great comedies [*Much Ado About Nothing, As You Like It,* and *Twelfth Night*] are even more exclusively the plays of lovers and their wooing than are the earlier ones, seldom does Shakespeare allow their wooing to express itself through the full gamut of its lyric modulations. Its utterance is adapted to a dramatic, and, indeed, to a comic scene: depth of affection is displayed rather by hints and by deeds than by the conventional phrase of the love poet. The homily of love from its gentle pulpiters is felt to be tedious, and is seldom allowed to weary its hearers. Often, indeed, when the wooing itself is an extended episode of the story, it is camouflaged in circumstances shaped by the wooers to cover their real passion. Beatrice and Benedick deliberately adopt a kind of inverted technique of love-making; and for them, the normal idiom of lovers is feigned by others so as to be overheard by the two who are to be the victims of the device. Rosalind, disguised as Ganymede, pretends to be herself in order to teach Orlando to woo. Viola expresses her own love by innuendo, and finds a sort of outlet for her inhibition, as well as a gratification for her own sense of restraint, in unfolding to Olivia the passion of the Duke's loves, as if hallooing her name to the reverberate hills to make the babbling gossip of the air cry out "Olivia." But hav-

"The Consummation" by H. B. Charlton. From ch. 9, "The Consummation," in Shakespearian Comedy (London: Methuen & Co., Ltd., 1938), pp. 277-297. Copyright 1938 by Methuen & Co., Ltd. Slightly abridged for this edition. Reprinted by permission of Methuen & Co., Ltd.

ing done this Viola will find it easier to be her natural self. "I took great pains to study it, and 'tis poetical." In the throes of her own love, she will revert to sanity. . . .

Rosalind, Viola, and to a less extent, Beatrice, are Shakespeare's images of the best way to love. They, and the men in whom they inspire love, are Shakespeare's representation of the office of love to lift mankind to a richer life. So, by the entry into it of love, not only has the world of these comedies become a bigger world: the men and women who inhabit it have become finer and richer representatives of human nature. They have entered into the possession of spiritual endowments which, if hitherto suspected to exist at all, had either been distrusted as dangerous or had become moribund through desuetude. They have claimed the intuitive, the subconscious, and the emotional as instruments by which personality may bring itself into a fuller consciousness of and a completer harmony with the realities of existence. They have left Theseus far behind; they have also outgrown Falstaff. . . .

Shakespeare's enthronement of woman as queen of comedy is no mere accident, and no mere gesture of conventional gallantry. Because they are women, these heroines have attributes of personality fitting them more certainly than men to shape the world towards happiness. His menfolk, a Hamlet or a Macbeth or an Othello, may have a subtler intellect, a more penetrating imagination, or a more irresistible passion. But what they have more largely in one kind of personal endowment, they own only at the expense of other properties no less essential to the encountering of such varied circumstances as are presented by the act of living. These heroes, in effect, are out of harmony with themselves, and so are fraught with the certainty of tragic doom. Their personality is a mass of mighty forces out of equipoise: they lack the balance of a durable spiritual organism. It was in women that Shakespeare found this equipoise, this balance which makes personality in action a sort of ordered interplay of the major components of human nature. In his women, hand and heart and brain are fused in a vital and practicable union, each contributing to the other, no one of them permanently pressing demands to the detriment of the other, yet each asserting itself periodically to exercise its vitality, even if the immediate effect be a temporary disturbance of equilibrium, for not otherwise will they be potent to exercise their proper function when the whole of their owner's spiritual nature is struck into activity. Perhaps it was primarily because Shakespeare found women more sensitive to intuition and more responsive to emotion that he first promoted them to dominion in the realm of comedy. He found, moreover, in their instincts a kind of finely developed mother wit, a variety of humanized common sense which, because it was impregnated with humane feeling, was more apt to lay hold of the essential realities of existence than was the more rarified and isolated intellect of man. But, though it was what to this extent may be called their essential femininity which gave his heroines their first claims to rulership in comedy, Shakespeare insisted in his maturest comedies that all the qualities which his heroines owed to the promptings of intuition and instinct were only certainly beneficent in human affairs when instinct and intuition were guided by a mind in which a sublimated common sense had established itself as the habitual director of action and behaviour.

It is unnecessary here to attempt to describe these heroines one by one, or even to name in detail all their generic traits. It will be enough to indicate one or two of their characteristic virtues. They have all the gift of inspiring and of returning affection. They have the good will of all who know them. They are simply human and patently natural in their response to emotional crises like that of falling in love. Rosalind's excitement when she first meets Orlando is as palpable as are her transparent endeavours to hide it. Their own passion still further sharpens the affection through which they seek the good of others. Once they are conscious of their own desire they are master-hands in reaching it. Rosalind is the main plotter of the flight to Arden; it is she who devises the means of ensuring Orlando's frequent company. Viola resolves at once to remedy her lot by taking service with the Duke; and immediately becomes his confidant and his private minister. She overcomes all the ceremonial obstacles which bar access to Olivia, using, when need be, the bluster and the rudeness which she learns from her opponents. She seizes a situation on the instant; and even when the outcome is not clearly to be foreseen, she acts in a manner which will save unnecessary suffering to others: "she took the ring of me," is her lie to Malvolio, guessing at once how the distraught Olivia had tried to hide her device from her steward and messenger. In crises, all of them, Rosalind, Viola, and Beatrice, are guided by intuitive insight. Beatrice acclaims Hero's innocence in the face of damning evidence. Viola judges her ship's captain by the same inner vision, and she confides in him implicitly. Yet the instinct and the intuition are always open-eyed and cautiously safeguarded against mere casual vagary or whimsical sentimentality. When Viola judges the captain's worth by his fair and outward character, she remembers that nature with a beauteous wall doth oft close in pollution. Rosalind and Celia are equally immune from this widespread romantic fallacy. They know that there is no certain and predictable relation between beauty and honesty in mankind: they would have laughingly recommended all the Tennysonian moralists of their day, who thought beauty to be either truth or virtue, to stroll through the equivalent of their West End after the theatres were shut and when the restaurants were coming to the end of their cabarets. Yet, with all the efficiency and savoir faire of which these heroines prove themselves to be possessed, they are amazingly modest. It is this modesty which prevents them from endeavoring to compass what is beyond mortal reach. Fortune, they know, is but a blind worker; and she doth most mistake in her gifts to woman. Viola undoubtedly is confident, but not over-confident: she will do what she can, but

> O time! thou must untangle this, not I;
> It is too hard a knot for me to untie.

And Rosalind never forgets how full of briers is this work-a-day world. But in the end, they triumph; and they triumph because they are just what they are, the peculiar embodiment in personality of those traits of human nature which render human beings most lovable, most loving, and most serviceable to the general good.

But these ladies are not only doers and inspirers of action. Merely by their presence in the play, they serve as standards whereby degrees of worth and worthlessness in other characters are made manifest. Hence the rich variety of theme, of episode, and of person in these plays is knit together and holds as a coherent structure. The beneficence of emotion and of intuition is no wise belittled by the revelation of the follies which spring from feeling in less stable creatures than are the heroines. So, *Twelfth Night* is largely occupied with the disclosure of unbalanced sentiment. There is the enervating sentimentality of Orsino, there is the unrestrained emotionalism of Olivia. *As You Like It* handles an allied theme by its exposure of merely conventional pastoralism. Indeed, once the positive construction of their larger world has been effected by the heroines, there is now place, not only for their own safeguards for it, such as this perpetual alertness to expose the dangers of unbalanced sentiment, there is also place for the sort of direct satire and the forthright comicality which were the manner of the older classical tradition. Just as Sir Toby finds his station in *Twelfth Night,* so do Andrew and even Malvolio; there, in Andrew's case, simply to display his own foolish inanity as do the witless in all sorts of comedy; and in Malvolio's, to enter almost as Jonson gave his characters entry, for a more subtle but still classical kind of discomfiture. As Malvolio in *Twelfth Night,* so Jaques in *As You Like It,* another of the few attempts of Shakespeare to project malcontentism for comic purposes. Besides these, traditional clowns may now also play their part, whether the English Shakespearian ones of the tribe of Bottom, such as Dogberry and Verges, or the more technical ones, Feste and Touchstone, grown now by contact with natural Costards into something more substantial and more homely than the mere tradi-

tional corrupters of words, and therefore playing not the part of an
added funny interlude, but an essential role in the orientation of the
idea of comedy. "Since the little wit that fools have was silenced, the
little foolery that wise men have makes a great show." The true fool's
return is restorative. A fool of his sort will use his folly like a stalking-
horse, and under the presentation of that, will shoot his wit. Yet his
range will necessarily be limited now. Only the crassest folly falls to
such arrows, for those who have become expert in human traffickings
can assume an easy indifference to simple and direct hits:

> He that a fool doth very wisely hit
> Doth very foolishly, although he smart,
> Not to seem senseless of the bob; if not,
> The wise man's folly is anatomized
> Even by the squandering glances of the fool.

Thus the motley of romantic comedies is subtler than the slapdash
skittle-knocking of the satire in classical comedy. Their reformatory
way, too, is fundamentally different from the simple exposure of ludicrous abnormality which had been the approved manner of older
comedy. They entice to a richer wisdom by alluring the imagination
into desire for larger delights. They are not mainly concerned to whip
offenders into conventional propriety by scorn and by mockery. They
persuade one to the better state by presenting it in all its attractiveness:
they depict a land of heart's desire, and, doing that, reveal the way of
human and natural magic by which it is to be attained.

Hence, in the last resort, the greatness of these greatest of Shakespeare's comedies will be measured by the profundity and the per-
suasiveness of the apprehension of life which they embody, by the
worth, that is, of their underlying worldly wisdom. What then is this
comic idea of which these plays are the dramatic revelation?

Something of the answer has already been given in estimating the
characteristics of the heroines. But the conclusions may be made more
general: in the first place, however, it must be noted that though these
romantic comedies break through the traditional scope of classical
comedy, their sphere is still rigorously confined within the proper orbit
of comedy. They limit themselves to acquaintance with life here and
now; the world, and not eternity, is their stage. It is, of course, a world
presenting many more woeful pageants than comedy is capable of
transmuting to happiness: and comedy must confine itself to those
threats of fate and those rubs of circumstance which can be reconciled
with man's reach for assured joy in living. In these ripest of Shakespeare's comedies, comedy is seeking in its own artistic way to elucidate
the moral art of securing happiness by translating the stubbornness of
fortune into a quiet and a sweet existence.

It finds that this art comes most easily to those who by nature are generous, guiltless, and of a free disposition, just, indeed, as are Shakespeare's heroines. It finds the art crippled, if not destroyed, in those who lack the genial sense of fellowship with mankind. A Malvolio, sick of self-love, thanking God that he is not of the element of his associates, sees the rest of men merely as specimens of the genus 'homo,'—"why, of mankind." The springs of sympathy are dried up within him. He becomes merely a timeserver, planning only for his own selfish gain. The aptitude to do this successfully had been a positive asset to the earlier, even to the Falstaffian, kind of comic hero. But now, in the radiance of these maturer plays, it is seen in truer light. Malvolio has lost the art of life; his very genius is infected. . . .

PART TWO

View Points

G. K. Hunter: Plot and Subplot in *Twelfth Night*

. . . The vision of happiness is thus for Viola a smiling through tears, a vision all the more poignant for its unlikeliness to be fulfilled. To say this is to make Viola sound like the archetype for much modern "brave little woman" sentimentality. And she is not: the play is too busy to let her seem so. The sentiment is placed in a current of cross-intrigues which keeps it from the stagnation of sentimentality. Happiness is a perpetual possibility which has to be shelved away as soon as it is exposed (for matters, not hostile, but more immediately pressing, always intervene); it is a single thread in a broadloom that is largely made up of threats and deceptions. It is one of the functions of the large-scale and fully developed subplot of this play to complicate each of the visits that Viola makes to the house of Olivia, and to cross-hatch the final comedy of errors between Sebastian and Viola.

But the complications introduced by the subplot are not to be limited to the intrigues it contains; what we have here is not a simple world of below-stairs bumbling and aping (as in *Much Ado*) but a real, even if easily deflected, threat to the security of princely natures and developed sensibilities. On the self-indulgence of Olivia and Orsino must be laid at least some of the blame for the presumptuousness of Malvolio and the idle mischief of Sir Toby. Malvolio's aspiration to join the aristocracy is not absurd; his disguise in smiles and yellow stockings can be seen as a nastier variant of the "mental disguise" of Orsino and Olivia—their willingness to act on temporary obsessions, and to forget the continuity of their lives. All are presented as victims of a need to hide from the isolated truth (and here Viola, though her disguise is forced on her and not chosen, must be joined with the others): Olivia cannot bear to be known for what she is—a healthy and nubile woman; Viola cannot permit herself to be known for what she is—a girl; Orsino cannot bear to be known for what he is—a lover in love with the idea of love; Sir Toby cannot bear to be known for a parasite, Sir Andrew for a fool, Malvolio for a steward. The process of the play is one which allows these truths to be bearable (or socially

"Plot and Subplot in Twelfth Night" by G. K. Hunter. From the section on Twelfth Night in Shakespeare: The Later Comedies, Writers and Their Works, No. 143, Longmans, Green & Co. Ltd., 1962, pp. 43-55. Copyright © 1962 by G. K. Hunter. Reprinted by permission of G. K. Hunter and Longmans, Green & Co. Ltd.

organized) at the end of the action, not by developing characters to a
greater understanding, but simply by moving the plot around till the
major characters each find themselves opposite a desirable partner and
an escape hatch from absurdity. The new pattern at the end is seen
not only as personally satisfying, but also as socially desirable, certain
pretenders to civility (notably Malvolio and Sir Andrew) being rejected from the pattern (as in Restoration Comedy), in which the
others express their own superior natures. It is true that there is a
degree of "Jonsonian" social realism in the play's image of an effete
aristocracy threatened by a determined upstart; the economic basis
of the relationship between Sir Toby and Sir Andrew is clearly stated
(II.iv.170 ff.), and the marriage of Sir Toby and Maria is more a piece
of social justice than a contribution to any final dance of reconciliation.
But this dance itself is not to be explained in social terms; the principal emotion involved in the denouement is the sense of release from
the complexity and isolation of outer disguise or inner obsession; and
this is a personal and individual matter, to which society is merely
accessary:

> When . . . golden time convents,
> A solemn combination shall be made
> Of our dear souls. Meantime, sweet sister,
> We will not part from hence. Cesario, come;
> For so you shall be, while you are a man;
> But when in other habits you are seen,
> Orsino's mistress, and his fancy's queen.   (V.i.368-74)

But we may well feel that the play has related the dream world of
"golden time" too securely to the class struggle around it to allow this
to be more than a partial reconciliation. The amount of space that the
denouement gives to Malvolio (about one hundred lines out of a
total of one hundred seventy-five) may seem to be indicative of Shakespeare's waning interest in these glamorous aristocrats. In *As You
Like It* the dance of lovers was broken by the solitary Jaques but was
not marred by him, for he too had found a milieu in which he could
be himself:

> [*to Duke*] You to your former honour I bequeath;
> Your patience and your virtue well deserves it.
> [*to Orlando*] You to a love that your true faith doth merit;
> . . .   So, to your pleasures:
> I am for other than for dancing measures.   (V.iv.180-87)

But the exit of Malvolio:

> I'll be reveng'd on the whole pack of you.   (V.i.364)

is more difficult to fit in. The Duke instructs servants to

> Pursue him, and entreat him to a peace,

but we are hardly convinced that this will be effective. The happiness
of the lovers would seem to have been bought at a price which ex-
cludes Malvolio, and we may feel that this circumscribes and diminishes
the final effect of their happiness. . . .

Harold C. Goddard: The Third Degree of . . .

. . . If ever there were mansions fading from excess, they were those
of Olivia and the Duke in this play, and that that is what Shakespeare
set out to show is strongly indicated by the opening and the close
of the piece (of its end we will speak at the end). Taken together they
practically prove as much. The familiar speech of the Duke with
which *Twelfth Night* opens is like a musical overture in which Shakespeare, as so often, announces his main theme:

> If music be the food of love, play on;
> Give me excess of it, that, surfeiting,
> The appetite may sicken, and so die.
> That strain again! It had a dying fall.
> . . . Enough, no more!
> 'Tis not so sweet now as it was before.

Excess! Surfeit! Sicken! Dying fall! Enough, no more! 'Tis not so sweet
now as it was before! Even at a second reading this play is not so
sweet as it was before—but it is more tartly significant. Pretty nearly
everybody in it but Viola and Sebastian—and those two outskirt characters, the sea captains—is at the extreme point where from excess of
something or other he is about to be converted into something else.
Sir Toby, who is the feudal retainer at his vanishing point, is in the
"third degree of drink," drowned in it, namely. (Those who liken him
to Falstaff are in some still higher degree of obfuscation.) Feste the
jester is in the third degree of "wit." (There is another wiser Feste,
emerging from the "dry" one like a butterfly from a chrysalis, of
whom we will speak later.) Sir Andrew is in the third, nay the nth,
degree of fatuity—the complete gentleman so attenuated that he is
indistinguishable from the complete fool. He is class transmigrated into
ass, with not "so much blood in his liver as will clog the foot of a flea."

*"The Third Degree of. . . ." by Harold C. Goddard. From "Twelfth Night," ch.
10 in* The Meaning of Shakespeare *(Chicago: The University of Chicago Press, 1951),
pp. 294-306. Copyright © 1951 by the University of Chicago Press. Reprinted by
permission of the University of Chicago Press.*

He is a great consumer of beef and thinks that life consists of eating and drinking—and pretending to fight. He is Sir Toby's gull, as Roderigo is Iago's.

Maria's third degree is of another sort. She is a lively, alert, resourceful mocking person. Her vitality and intelligence (to call it that) have, in her servile position, made her ambitious and envious, especially so of the steward whose merits her mistress prizes so highly. It is important to realize that it is not just because he is Malvolio that she hates him. She would have resented anyone in his place. "I can hardly forbear hurling things at him." The remark is a giveaway. There is a vague premonition of the Iago-Cassio theme here on the comic level as her simile, "I have dogged him like his murderer," is enough to show. Her "humor" is of that low order that must always have a physical outlet. She has her jests, she says, at her fingers' ends (not at her tongue's). She will make her fellow conspirators laugh themselves into stitches. Her sport must always bear immediate fruit that others can see and feel. In this case to show off her talents before Sir Toby is as strong a motive as to humiliate Malvolio. She tickles and catches her trout. And Toby rewards her by asking, "Wilt thou set thy foot o' my neck?" (which she doubtless did with a vengeance after they were married) and calling her "thou most excellent devil of wit!" What wonder that in her the spirit of fun passes from the cathartic prank of the cross garters and yellow stockings to the cruel and perilous practical joke of the dark room. Fabian and finally Sir Toby himself see that they have gone too far. But Maria plainly means it when she says that if Malvolio really does go mad, it will be well worth it: the house will be the quieter! There is a cruel streak in her as there generally is in practical jokers. She is in that third degree of fun where what might originally have been a sense of humor becomes perverted and commits suicide. But her excesses will trouble few people in the theater. They have made them laugh too heartily. . . .

Alan S. Downer: Feste's Exposure of Orsino

. . . But, if we have been beguiled by our own sentimentality into sympathy with the Duke, Feste will set us right, and most particularly in that romantic scene (II, 4) where he has been thrust in to sing the song which Viola seems not prepared to perform.[1] It is as early in the

"Feste's Exposure of Orsino" by Alan S. Downer. From "Feste's Night," College English, XIII (1952), 258-265. Copyright © 1952 by the University of Chicago Press. Reprinted by permission of Alan S. Downer and the University of Chicago Press.

[1] There has been much ingenuity expended on the search for an explanation for

morning as the love-smitten Duke would arise from bed. He enters, calling at once for music, and requests Cesario (that is, Viola) for that "old and antique song" they heard last night. While his servant Curio goes in search of Feste to sing it, Orsino proceeds to analyze it for us. The description is famous and explicit:

> It is old and plain,
> The spinsters and the knitters in the sun,
> And the free maids that weave their thread with bones,
> Do use to chant it. It is silly sooth,
> And dallies with the innocence of love
> Like the old age.   (II.iv.44-49)

That is, a simple song, presumably a folk song or ballad, fit accompaniment to a household task. It is a love song, but not impassioned, not from the point of view of fervent youth. It dallies with the harmless pleasure of love as if the experience were but the memory of the old, a memory recollected in tranquillity. Whereupon Feste sings:

> Come away, come away, death,
>   And in sad cypress let me be laid.
> Fly away, fly away, breath;
>   I'm slain by a fair cruel maid.
> My shroud of white, stuck all with yew,
>   O prepare it!
> My part of death, no one so true
>   Did share it.

In the second stanza the love imagery becomes more extravagant.

> Not a flower, not a flower sweet,
>   On my black coffin let there be strown;
> Not a friend, not a friend greet
>   My poor corpse, where my bones shall be thrown.
> A thousand, thousand sighs to save,
>   Lay me, O where
> Sad, true lover ne'er find my grave,
>   To weep there.

---

this awkward *non sequitur*. Possibly, we are dealing with a revision of the text in which the boy new-cast for Viola was less versatile than his predecessor. In that case the present interpretation is a further demonstration of the playwright's skill in making a virtue of necessity. It is intriguing also to speculate that, since Feste sings all the other songs in the play, Shakespeare in revising took this opportunity of tightening up his structure. But, barring the resurrection of Ireland or Collier, proof for such hypotheses can never be forthcoming, and, however happily we would welcome it, it is of secondary importance in dealing with a work of art as an entity in itself.

Without the original music, which cannot be traced, it is impossible
to say for certain, but, from the striking difference between the song
as anticipated and the song as sung, Feste seems to have been mocking,
indirectly, the Duke's passion. "Come away, death" is indeed a love
song, but it can hardly be said to dally with the innocence of love. This
would explain the Duke's abrupt, "There's for thy pains," and his
immediate dismissal, not only of the singer,[2] but of his entire court.
Perhaps he is afraid that there may have been some sniggering behind
his back as Feste sang. There is just a hint in the play that his household is a little wearied of his unavailing pursuit of Olivia. . . .

Mark Van Doren: Sir Toby Belch and His Milieu

. . . Sir Toby Belch is a gentleman too, or at any rate he belongs. He
is an old relation and retainer in the somewhat cluttered household of
Olivia. *The Merchant of Venice* never took us so deep into domestic
details. The household of Olivia is old-world, it is Merry England.
At its center sits the lady Olivia, but there is room for every other
kind of person here for whom a changing age has still not made existence impossible. There is the clown Feste and the clever servant
Fabian; and there is the still cleverer servant Maria, whose extreme
smallness is rendered clear to us, in the perverse language of a good-
natured people, by such terms as "giant" and "Penthesilea," though
she is also a "wren" and "a little villain." Chiefly, however, there is Sir
Toby. He is gluttonous and drunken, and must be kept out of sight
as much as possible; but Olivia would no more turn him away than
she would refuse to hear an excellent old song sung to the lute. For
one thing there is no place for Sir Toby to go. He is as old-fashioned
as Falstaff, and as functionless in the modern world. "Am not I consanguineous? Am I not of her blood?" (II.iii.82-3). He even talks like
Falstaff, puffingly and explosively, as he reminds Maria that he is
Olivia's uncle. And for another thing he belongs. Old households
harbor such old men. They are nuisances to be endured because they
are symbols of enduringness, signs of the family's great age. Sir Toby
has another parasite on him—Sir Andrew Aguecheek, whose foolish
devotion to Olivia he makes use of to keep himself in money. For of

---

"Sir Toby Belch and His Milieu" by Mark Van Doren. From the chapter on
Twelfth Night *in* Shakespeare *(Doubleday-Anchor reprint, 1955), pp. 135-143. Copy-
right 1939, © 1967 by Mark Van Doren. Reprinted by permission of Holt, Rinehart
& Winston, Inc.*

[2] With a formula which is exactly duplicated only in Henry IV's angry dismissal
of his insubordinate nobles.

course he has no money; and Sir Andrew has a little. It is a crowded household, swarming with gross life behind high walls of custom. When Sir Andrew says he is of the opinion that life consists of eating and drinking, Sir Toby applauds him roundly. "Thou'rt a scholar; let us therefore eat and drink" (II.iii.13-4). The fat old fellow's second appearance in the play (I.v.129-30) brings him on belching—"a plague o' these pickle-herring!" And he is ever as full of wine as he is loud with song. "How now, sot!" "Shall we make the welkin dance indeed? Shall we rouse the night-owl in a catch that will draw three souls out of one weaver? Shall we do that?" (II.iii.58-61).

It is to Sir Toby that Malvolio is most alien. "Dost thou think, because thou art virtuous, there shall be no more cakes and ale?" This most famous sentence in the play is more than Sir Toby disposing of his niece's steward; it is the old world resisting the new, it is the life of hiccups and melancholy trying to ignore latter-day puritanism and efficiency. On the occasion when it is spoken there is danger for Sir Toby in the fact that Olivia is moody with her new love for Cesario; she has lost patience with her kinsman's misdemeanors, and may send him off. But Malvolio is the last man on earth to come with the message. "Tell us something of him," says Sir Toby to Maria.

> *Maria.* Marry, sir, sometimes he is a kind of puritan.
> *Sir Andrew.* O, if I thought that, I'd beat him like a dog!
> *Sir Toby.* What, for being a puritan? Thy exquisite reason, dear knight?
> *Sir Andrew.* I have no exquisite reason for't, but I have reason good
> enough.   (II.iii.151-8)

So has Sir Toby, though neither of them is articulate enough to say what it is. Doubtless they have never thought it out. They only knew that the sight of Malvolio, like the sound of his voice, threatens death to their existence. His own existence somehow challenges their right to be freely what they are. He is of a new order—ambition, self-contained, cold and intelligent, and dreadfully likely to prevail. That is why Sir Toby and his retinue hate him. Feste at the end provides too simple an explanation. The humiliation of Malvolio, he says, was his personal revenge upon one who had discounted him to his mistress as "a barren rascal," a jester unworthy of his hire. But the others had been as active as Feste, and they had had no such motive. "The devil a puritan that he is," Maria insists, "or anything constantly, but a time-pleaser; an affection'd ass" (II.iii.159-60). Puritan or not, Malvolio has offended them as a class. They could have forgiven his being a clincher, his having affection for himself, if he had been any other kind of man than the cool kind he is. . . .

W. Moelwyn Merchant: Theological Punning in *Twelfth Night*

. . . *Twelfth Night* is especially interesting. Among the central themes of the comedy the "theological" moments are barely more than asides, but they carry far more than their bulk would suggest. The witty deflation of Olivia's pretentious and posturing decision to mourn her brother depends on a double play on the nature of tears—her "eye-offending brine" will be both a ceremonial aspersing of her chamber twice a day with holy water (whose composition by the addition of salt gives rise to the regular punning association of eyes and tears with stoups and holy water) and a preservation of her brother's memory ("to *season* her dead brother's love") as beef is preserved in brine for the winter. The wittily irreverent use of sacrament or ceremony in association with a domestic commonplace is a secure element in the "metaphysical" tradition and can appear without discomfort only among a circle or in a period when theology is accepted or assumed with assured familiarity. Feste's excursions into social criticism are regularly given substance by his scriptural or theological asides; one of the most extended puns in fact carries little serious weight but establishes this kind of relationship between his vocabulary and Maria's. At one of his delinquencies, with Maria's warning that he will be hanged for it, Feste declares that "he that is well hanged need fear no colour"; Maria's challenge to "make that good" produces the apparently lame reply that "he shall see none to fear," which Maria amplifies to the seemingly weak, "a good lenten answer." In fact they are playing with the commonplaces of liturgical practice, since the church of Shakespeare's day used as the liturgical "colour" for Lent not the purple or violet of the Roman use but the "Lenten array" of unbleached linen, literally "no colour." It is in this temper that serious moments elsewhere in the play are carried so lightly, with references to "Brownists" and "politicians," to the moral casuistry of the breeding of coins, and to the darker questions of feigning appearance and hypocrisy which never become morally oppressive in the handling. Similarly, at the opening of *As You Like It*, references to the Prodigal Son ("keep your hogs and eat husks," "prodigal portion," "elder brother," "the poor allottery my father left me by testament") add substance and weight to the fairy tale quality which Professor Harold Jenkins so lucidly argues. . . .

"Theological Punning in Twelfth Night" *by W. Moelwyn Merchant. From* "Shakespeare's Theology," Review of English Literature, *V (1964), 72-88. Copyright © 1964 by Longmans, Green & Co., Ltd. Reprinted by permission of W. Moelwyn Merchant and Longmans, Green & Co., Ltd.*

Leslie Hotson: Punning in Feste's Final Song

. . . To close up the Illyrian revel with music and moral, Shakespeare gives us Feste's celebrated song, *When that I was and a little tiny boy.* For lack of understanding of its drift, this song has naïvely been received as a tale in rime but little reason: nonsense contemptible or nonsense charming; but nonsense. But is Feste the man to waste his wit in nonsense? He knows precisely what to provide as a fitting farewell to wassail and saturnalian excess: and it is not something adapted to a Christmas party for Victorian young persons. As Rupert Brooke observed, "the Elizabethans liked obscenity; and the primness and the wickedness that do not like it, have no business with them."

Must we really be reminded that ribaldry was the proper and age-old function of the Fool? Shakespeare's colleague Robert Armin played not only Feste but Lear's Fool as well. Knavish, licentious speech is common to both roles; and Armin's rendering of Feste's song proved so popular that an additional stanza was sung in *Lear—He that has and a little tiny wit.* Historically, the Fool and indecency cannot be parted. To make up for his mental shortcomings, Nature was commonly believed to have endowed the Fool with an excess of virility, symbolized by his *bauble.* "Fools please women best." "A fool's bauble is a lady's playfellow." "A foolish bed-mate, why he hath no peer." Priapus used to be described as *that foolish god;* and Mercutio's cynical notion of Love is a *great natural* with his *bauble.*

Feste's lascivious lapses earn him Lady Olivia's sharp reproof—"you grow dishonest." We realize that he has not forgotten its sting, when, with the Fool's immemorial trick of "box about"—that is, of passing a received blow on to someone else—he buffets the devil of lechery in Malvolio with this same *dishonest:* "Talkest thou nothing but of ladies? . . . Fie, thou dishonest Satan!" His boastful pun, "He that is *well hang'd* [i.e., *handsomely furnished or adorned with virility*] in this world, needs to fear no colours [*no deceptions or foes*]" is taken up by Maria.[1] She tells him, "Make that good [*Prove that* statement in

"Punning in Feste's Final Song" by Leslie Hotson. From "Illyria for Whitehall," ch. 7 in The First Night of Twelfth Night *(New York: The Macmillan Company, 1955; London: Rupert Hart-Davis Ltd., 1955), pp. 151-172. Copyright © 1954 by Leslie Hotson. Reprinted by permission of Leslie Hotson and the publishers.*

[1] For this sense of *hang'd,* see the fool Pompey in Fletcher and Massinger's *Wit at Several Weapons,* 2.2: "When they saw how I was hang'd . . ." Compare Cotgrave's translation of *Couillatris:* "Well hang'd." Maria gives Feste the derivation of his byword: "I can tell where that saying was born, of 'I fear no colors' . . . In the wars." *Colors* of course means "military colors" as well as "deceptions." The historical source would seem to be *La Guerre Folle* or the Mad War of 1485 in France. Sir Walter Raleigh, writing on the valor of the English fighting man, lifts a sig-

a decent sense]." And Feste's lenten answer blandly reverts to the dismal but innocent gallows-meaning: a man well hang'd *by that neck* "shall see none to fear."

As for Lear's Fool, he advertises the Fool's characteristic advantage by announcing, "Marry, here's grace and a codpiece: that's a wise man and a fool." To this he adds a complacent boast of his physical irresistibility to the other sex: "ladies too, they will not let me have all the fool to myself, they'll be snatching." [2] And he closes the first act of the tragedy with the witty and bawdy tag

> She that's a maid now, and laughs at my *deporter,*
> Shall not be a maid long, unless things be cut shorter.

The text has *departure,* a word unacceptable both for the rime and for the sense. I suggest that Shakespeare must have written *deporter,* which Cotgrave gives as the French for "a sporting bauble." What roused the wanton wench to hilarity was not the Fool's vanishing but the sight of his immoderate "bauble." [3] *Thing* in its "bauble" sense is the key word, not only here, but also in the first stanza of Feste's song. In the Fool's childish state as a little tiny boy, a *foolish thing* was no more than a harmless trifle. Far otherwise, however, when he was grown "fit for breed"—a lecherous knave and thief of love, on the prowl after other men's wives:

> 'Gainst knaves and thieves men shut their gate.

Having begun by making sure that in listening to Feste's song we are not like that blockish Rosencrantz, with whom a knavish speech

---

nificant incident from Jean de Serre's French History: "Or I may cite another place of the same Authour, where hee tells, how the *Britons* [i.e., Bretons], being invaded by *Charles* the eight, King of France, thought it good policie, to apparell a thousand and two hundred of their owne men in *English* Cassacks; hoping that the very sight of the English red Crosse, would be enough to terrifie the *French.*"— *The Historie of the World.* Another writer, Henry Belasyse, employed the same familiar incident, as follows: "These victoryes [in the Hundred Years' War] made the English so famous, that the Duke of Britanny warring against Charles 8th of France, to strike terror into the French, apparelled fifteen hundred of his owne subjects in English armes and under the English colours. But the asse is never the better for having putt on the lyons skinne, nor Britons [Bretons] for appearing like English."—H.M.C., *Various,* 2.196. Feste may be bold to use a phrase extolling the terrific reputation of English military valour.

[2] Compare the Fool's song in *Volpone,* 1.2.71:
> Your Fool, he is your great man's darling,
> And your ladies' sport and pleasure;
> Tongue and bauble are his treasure.

[3] "Shee is enamour'd on the fooles bable" *Jack Drum's Entertainment* (1600), Act 2, line 308.

sleeps in a foolish ear, we may now look at the "reason of the rime"
—the plan of the ditty as a whole. Feste has already given us his ex-
quisite love songs; now we are to be sent away with "a song of good
life." What he trolls out is a Drunkard's Progress, an Elizabethan
forerunner of such bibulous confessions as *I'm a rambling wreck of
poverty* and *I've been a moonshiner for seventeen long years:* a moral
and musical reminder that the wassailing of the Twelfth Night
saturnalia had better not be followed as a way of life. That is the road
to "wet damnation." He has already told Lady Olivia—as they con-
template the condition of Sir Toby—that a drunken man is like a fool,
a madman, and a drowned man: "One draught above heat makes him
a fool, the second mads him, and third drowns him." Now he proceeds
to illustrate, with a dramatic lyric a rueful reminiscence leading us
through the same three familiar degrees—goat-drunk, lion-drunk, and
swine-drunk: "now goatishly to whore, now lion-like to roar, now
hoggishly in the mire"—whose attendant deadly sins, appropriated to
the three ages of manhood (youth, prime, and old age), are Lechery,
Wrath, and Sloth.

As we have noticed, in the second stanza—*'Gainst knaves and thieves
men shut their gate*—the lecherous knave finds that his goatish vice
renders him an outcast, shut out in the rain. In the third stanza, un-
able to mend his ways on the precept "Leave thy drink and thy whore,
and keep in-a-door," he makes a shiftless, beggarly, wrangling marriage.
Lion-drunk, he dings the pots about, swaggers with his own shadow,
and his screeching wife drives him forth—out in the rain.

The final phase exhibits him in the torpor, the "benumbing
apoplectic sleep" of the swine-drunk—*But when I came unto my
beds. Beds* is inevitably plural: the various spots where he happened to
fall. The abandoned drunkard has many beds, as well as a long series
of drunken heads in toss-pot company. As John Day puts it, "The last
. . . carry their beds o' their backs . . . and go to bed in the kennel
. . . and these we call Swine-drunk."[4] The grovelling Sly of *The
Taming of the Shrew* is either hog or corpse: "This were a bed but
cold to sleep so soundly. O monstrous beast! How like a swine he lies!
Grim death, how foul and loathsome is thine image!"

Again, out in the rain. "Through the sharp hawthorn blows the
cold wind." With a sorrowful hey-ho, the wind and the rain, and the
implied early death they bring with them, form the inevitable burden.
A great while ago the world begun;[5] and for the drunken fool without
the wit to come in out of the rain, it is all but ended. What of it?
But that's all one. . . . Then turning smoothly into Robin Armin the

[4] "Peregrinatio Scholastica" *Works* (ed. Bullen, 1880), 51, 52.
[5] Feste's "A great while ago the world begun" recalls the Elizabethan euphemism
for coition, "To dance The Beginning of the World."

player, Feste is out of his moral and into an Epilogue, to beg a gracious
plaudite of the hearers—

> our Play is done,
> And we'll strive to please you every day.

Chronology of Important Dates

	Shakespeare	*Historical and Cultural Events*
1564	(April 26) Christened at Stratford.	Christopher Marlowe born.
1577-80		Drake circumnavigated the world.
1582	(November) Married to Anne Hathaway.	
1583	(May 26) Daughter, Susanna, christened.	
1584-87		Raleigh's three attempts to colonize Virginia.
1585	(February 2) The twins, Hamnet and Judith, christened.	
1587		Mary, Queen of Scots, executed.
1588-92	Early plays being performed in London.	Spanish Armada defeated (1588).
1589		Publication of *The Faerie Queene* (1589-96).
1592	Attacked posthumously by Robert Greene.	Death of Montaigne.
1593-94	Dedication of *Venus and Adonis* and *The Rape of Lucrece* to Southampton.	
1594	Membership in the Lord Chamberlain's company of actors.	Henry IV crowned King of France.
1596	Death of son, Hamnet.	
1597	Bought New Place in Stratford.	First edition of Bacon's *Essays*.
1598		First seven books of Chapman's translation of the *Iliad* published.

	Shakespeare	*Historical and Cultural Events*
1599-1600	*As You Like It, Twelfth Night.*	Globe Theatre built (1599).
1600-1609	The major tragedies performed.	
1603		Death of Elizabeth I; accession of James I.
1611-13	Retired to Stratford.	First edition of the Authorized (King James) Version of the Bible (1611).
1616	(April 23) Died at Stratford.	Jonson published folio edition of his works.
1620		Pilgrims landed at Plymouth Rock.
1623	First Folio edition of Shakespeare's plays.	

Notes on the Editor and Contributors

WALTER N. KING, the editor of this volume, is Professor of English at the University of Montana. He has published articles on Shakespeare, Elizabethan rhetoric, and Shaw.

C. L. BARBER is Professor of English at the New York State University, Buffalo. His publications include, in addition to *Shakespeare's Festive Comedies* (1959), studies of Marlowe and Milton.

SYLVAN BARNET is Professor and Chairman of the Department of English of Tufts University. He is General Editor of the Signet Classic Shakespeare.

H. B. CHARLTON was Professor of English at the University of Manchester. His *Shakespearian Comedy* (1938) and *Shakespearian Tragedy* (1949) have been widely read for many years.

ALAN S. DOWNER is Professor and Chairman of the Department of English of Princeton University. He has written and edited many books on American, British, and Modern Drama, among them *The Theatre of Bernard Shaw* (1961).

HAROLD C. GODDARD was some years ago President of Swarthmore College and Professor of English. *The Meaning of Shakespeare* (1951) was published posthumously.

JOHN HOLLANDER is Professor of English at Hunter College. In 1958 he received the Yale Series of Younger Poets Award. His scholarly publications include *The Untuning of the Sky* (1961).

LESLIE HOTSON is a widely known literary historian and biographer. His many publications include *The Death of Christopher Marlowe* (1925), *Shakespeare's Sonnets Dated* (1949) and *Mr. W. H.* (1964).

G. K. HUNTER is Professor of English at the University of Warwick. His publications include his edition of the new Arden edition of *All's Well That Ends Well* (1959) and *John Lyly: The Humanist as Courtier* (1962).

CLIFFORD LEECH is Professor and Chairman of the Department of English of University College, University of Toronto. His publications in Elizabethan and Jacobean drama include *John Ford and the Drama of His Times* (1957) and *The John Fletcher Plays* (1962).

JULIAN MARKELS is Associate Professor of English at Ohio State University. He is presently engaged in a study of *Antony and Cleopatra*.

W. MOELWYN MERCHANT is Professor of English at the University of Exeter. In addition to numerous articles he has published *Shakespeare and the Artist* (1959) and edited *The Merchant of Venice* (1966) and *Edward II* (1967).

L. G. SALINGAR is a Fellow of Trinity College, Cambridge, and University Lecturer in English, Cambridge. In addition to articles written for the Pelican *Guide to English Literature,* he has recently published an essay on *The Revenger's Tragedy* (1965).

JOSEPH H. SUMMERS is Professor of English at Michigan State University. His publications include *George Herbert: His Religion and Art* (1954) and *The Muses' Method: an Introduction to Paradise Lost* (1962). He has also edited the Laurel *Marvell: Selected Poems* (1961).

MARK VAN DOREN, poet and critic, is Professor Emeritus of English at Columbia University. His critical works include *John Dryden, a Study of His Poetry* (1961) and *The Happy Critic and Other Essays* (1961).

PORTER WILLIAMS, JR., is Professor of English at the University of North Carolina. A recent publication is an essay on Conrad's *The Secret Sharer* (1964).

Selected Bibliography

Bethell, S. L., *Shakespeare and the Popular Dramatic Tradition* (London: King and Staples, 1944), pp. 33-34, 137-144. Incisive discussion of possible revision in the play.

Bradbrook, Muriel C., *The Growth and Structure of Elizabethan Comedy* (London: Chatto & Windus, Ltd., 1935; Penguin-Peregrine reprint, 1963). Excellent background study of the dramatic nexus out of which Shakespearian comedy developed.

Brown, John Russell, *Shakespeare and his Comedies* (London: Methuen & Co., Ltd., 1957). Detailed study of the comedies in line with four major concepts Brown singles out for special attention: love's wealth, love's truth, love's order, and love's ordeal.

Cecil, Lord David, *The Fine Art of Reading and Other Literary Studies* (London: Constable & Co., Ltd., 1957; New York: The Bobbs-Merrill Company, Inc., 1957), pp. 94-106. An acute analysis of Malvolio, Sir Andrew Aguecheek, and Feste.

Crane, Milton, "Twelfth Night and Shakespearian Comedy," *Shakespeare Quarterly*, VI (1955), 1-8. A good short study of the play's plot structure.

Draper, John W., *The Twelfth Night of Shakespeare's Audience* (Stanford: Stanford University Press, 1950). A study of the play as social comedy, one of its emphases being Shakespeare's realism in setting and characterization.

March, Ngaio, "A Note on a Production of *Twelfth Night*," *Shakespeare Survey 8* (1953), 69-73. A lively account of one modern production of the play in which strong effort was made to reconcile sixteenth and twentieth century values.

Mueschke, Paul, and Jeannette Fleisher, "Jonsonian Elements in the Comic Underplot of *Twelfth Night*," *Publications of the Modern Language Association*, XLVIII (1933), 720-740. A study of the influence of the humour characters of Ben Johnson upon the farcical comic characters in the play.

Nagarajan, S., " 'What You Will': A Suggestion," *Shakespeare Quarterly*, X (1959), 61-67. A short introduction into possible philosophical interpretations of the play.

Welsford, Enid, *The Fool: His Social and Literary History* (London: Faber & Faber, Ltd., 1935; New York: Doubleday & Company, Inc., [Anchor reprint], 1961), pp. 253-255. Feste's place within the Elizabethan tradition of the Fool is discussed along with his role within the play.

TWENTIETH CENTURY VIEWS

British Authors

TWENTIETH CENTURY VIEWS

European Authors